Tony Trigilio's *Craft: A Memoir* is an uncommon and entirely compelling exploration of influences, how what we read and where we place our attention determines the writing we produce. From meditation and mindfulness to the metaphysical and mysterious, Trigilio's clear and helpful advice for writers rightly encourages us to cast our vision "both wide and deep." Not your usual craft guide, but something even better.   **—DINTY W. MOORE**

When Trigilio tells you his poetry often takes place in the abandoned televangelist theme park of his childhood, take him at his word. Beginners reading this book with a sense of what Trigilio calls "obstinacy" will see a path to shape all of their passions toward creating art. The presiding spirits—it's fair to call them that—are his fellow writer Mitch, and Trigilio's cranky, half-feral cat Shimmy. (Mitch taught Tony to take himself seriously, and Shimmy had "untamed" opinions about Donald Rumsfeld and Glenn Beck.) Trigilio addresses both beginners and veterans, all of whom are always trying to incorporate "what I'm thinking about right now" into crafted writing. One overarching purpose of *Craft: A Memoir* is to communicate how he learned to internalize the outer world through wedding documentary impulse to his private inner landscape, and equally the contrary—to externalize his otherwise isolate inner world, manifested in poetry. Because Mitch and Shimmy are accompanied here by Tony's deceased parents, this is a book of the dead about how to make your writing live. You can't read it without wanting to start writing your own. MFA students, asked what they want more of in programs I've been associated with, always say craft; regardless of genre, here's a new book for them.

—DIANA HUME GEORGE

With horror, I learned from Tony Trigilio's *Craft: A Memoir* that Audubon shot and killed all the birds he'd depicted in his paintings! I don't know if I can forgive Trigilio for that bit of too-much-information, even though he says he was horrified, too. But I highlight that element that obnoxiously lingers like Disney's "It's A Small World" tune because it's a detail that's relevant for one of the most important ways to be a good poet: reading widely. (And Trigilio passed on the Audubon revelation from his own reading habits.) There are many "craft" lessons for this art of poetry which contains many paths. Trigilio's way includes knowing not only what one is supposed to know but also what he calls "arcane." By delivering his ideas convincingly, and with his own life as proof, he makes this book a worthwhile read.

—EILEEN R. TABIOS

In *Craft: A Memoir*, Tony Trigilio provides an inside look into his progression as a poet—from a "middling, utilitarian, rust-belt" childhood to an accomplished professor of creative writing. With side steps into journalism and music, Trigilio's true north remains poetry. He learns about craft and persistence from his teachers (Ms. Omark—4th grade) and his college profs and his grad school roommate Mitch Evich whose rigorous routine allows him to finish his novel. Trigilio continues to practice discipline and time-management alongside his wife Liz, also a writer. He meditates and keeps a journal. As he chronicles his own projects—from pop culture to history—Trigilio gives us a behind-the-desk view of one of our most celebrated American poets. A fascinating read.

—DENISE DUHAMEL

CRAFT: A MEMOIR

Craft: A Memoir

Tony Trigilio

MARSH HAWK PRESS · 2023
East Rockaway, New York

Marsh Hawk books are published by Marsh Hawk Press, Inc.,
a not-for-profit corporation under section 501(c)3
United States Internal Revenue Code.

Cover art & design: Michael Trigilio
Interior design & typesetting: Mark Melnick

FIRST EDITION
Library of Congress Cataloging-in-Publication Data

Names: Trigilio, Tony, 1966- author.
Title: Craft : a memoir / Tony Trigilio.
Description: First edition. | East Rockaway : Marsh Hawk Press, Inc., 2023.
Identifiers: LCCN 2022052196 | ISBN 9781732614178 (paperback)
Subjects: LCSH: Trigilio, Tony, 1966- | Poets, American--21st century--Biography. |
LCGFT: Autobiographies.
Classification: LCC PS3620.R546 Z46 2023 | DDC 811/.6
[B]--dc23/eng/20221028
LC record available at https://lccn.loc.gov/2022052196

Publication of this title was made possible in part by a regrant awarded
and administered by the Community of Literary Magazines and Presses (CLMP).
CLMP's NYS regrant programs are made possible by the New York State Council on
the Arts with the support of Governor Kathy Hochul and the New York State Legislature.

Marsh Hawk Press
P.O. Box 206, East Rockaway, N.Y. 11518-0206
mheditor@marshhawkpress.org

For Mitch Evich

Contents

ACKNOWLEDGMENTS

My thanks to the editors of the following journals and anthologies where versions of some of these chapters originally appeared in very different forms: *Big Other*, *On Becoming a Poet*, *Poets on Teaching*, and *Writers and Their Notebooks*. Deep gratitude to everyone at Marsh Hawk Press, especially Sandy McIntosh and Susan Terris. Warmest thanks to Jan Bottiglieri, Chris Green, Shelly Hubman, John Madera, Dale Moyer, Diana Raab, Liz Shulman, Michael Trigilio, and David Trinidad.

Passing Through Our Brief Moment in Time

Poetic language is the only kind of discourse that helps me untangle what is strange, weird, and sublime in my everyday lived experience. Poetry forces me to pay attention. It requires me to slow down my emotional and intellectual attention spans and listen to what the unknown world is telling me. But I also write from deep anxiety that some part of my environment might go unrepresented unless shaped into language.

The relationship between anxiety and speech was an inescapable part of my childhood. I was fortunate to grow up in a household and extended family where two different languages were spoken—English and Italian. I was exposed at any early age to the way language can fail to convey anything. What's more, my mother suffered from a severe hearing disorder, a malady that runs in our entire family, and we all took for granted that no matter how earnestly we try to communicate, our words inevitably leave gaps in understanding. Instead, each effort to try to represent a feeling, idea, or experience in language became something of a dare. As much as we distrusted language in my family, we just as fervently believed in it. We didn't need to read Wallace Stevens to know that words are "necessary fictions."

Language was and is our ticket into community. In my family, narrative was what kept us thriving. As a child, I was riveted by the colloquial oral histories my mother and father told over dinner—stories of how their first-generation immigrant families navigated the bizarre ways of this new country and how their otherness frustrated them. My impulse for narrative comes from my family's stories. But poetic narrative encompasses more than just plot-based storytelling that builds toward cleanly structured epiphanies. Poetic narrative is cross-cut with associational, often interfering images and phrases, and by counterpoint rhythms and voicings that interrupt the trajectory of the standard narrative arc. This dance between narrative linearity and flash-cut interruption is what makes the most opaque or elusive experiences speakable.

Like many poets, my first experience with this kind of discourse occurred in sacred texts, where the representation of extrasensory phenomena depends on the figurative language of poetry. Consider Ezekiel: the more you try to describe the flaming chariot you see in the sky, its wheel rims full of eyes, the stranger and more unfamiliar—and more poetic—your language becomes.

My first secular poetry obsession was Dylan Thomas, whose work taught me that poems express what can't be contained by the limited logic of everyday language. Like the religious texts of my Catholic childhood, Thomas's work induced a feeling of vertigo that, paradoxically, also helped me see the world more clearly—that encouraged me to pay attention to the ineffable landscapes beneath the surface of things. I couldn't take vision for granted anymore. Seeing was a matter of urgency.

"Begotten, not made, one in Being with the Father," we recited from the Nicene Creed each week in Catholic mass, describing the mystery of the incarnation—a line that I couldn't stop saying out loud when I was younger, even though it bewildered me to no end. Its regular rhythm clashed with its sinewy semantics, which heightened the difficulty of imagining the god-made-flesh we were celebrating in church every Sunday. Eventually, I decided that this line from the

Nicene Creed was the only appropriate verse to follow the opening lines of Thomas's "Altarwise by Owl-Light," one of the favorite poems of my youth (possibly because it was absolutely inscrutable to me): "Altarwise by owl-light in the half-way house / The gentleman lay graveward with his furies / Begotten, not made, one in Being with the Father."

I was thrilled by my earliest exposure to religious texts, but poetry was special because it was *secular*. Thomas's difficult, mystical poems weren't trying to persuade me to be a good Catholic, which would've been a futile effort, anyway. I converted to Buddhism a quarter-century ago, a religion with its own tradition of voicing what seems beyond language (but without the metaphysical doom and gloom of original sin).

Music was the bridge between religious language and poetry for me. The lyrics in songs like "Eleanor Rigby" and "Nowhere Man," especially, offered a vocabulary to describe the solitary nature of being human, a difficult feeling I was just starting to experience, and one that I barely understood. These songs suggested, as religious texts did, that a luminosity can be found inside those intensified moments of feeling when we are alone with ourselves.

You see, I grew up in a middling, utilitarian, rust-belt city, Erie, Pennsylvania. It was not the kind of place where you could find a lot of artistic role models. I was grateful for those rare moments when an adult asked me what I was writing and actually wanted to hear my answer. The first to do this was my fourth-grade writing teacher, Ms. Omark. She convinced me that I could write autobiographical material that other people might want to read. I composed my first serious poem in 1974, age eight, an anxiety-ridden response to my abject fear of tornadoes. We didn't have a basement. I wrote about my terror that we had nowhere to hide if a tornado touched down in our neighborhood. Ms. Omark liked the poem so much that she asked me to rewrite it on poster board and taped it to the front of her desk.

Later, in my first undergraduate poetry workshop at Kent State University, I began to take poetry seriously. We had little space in our family to cultivate the arts. But here I was, in a college-level classroom with twelve students who wanted to write poetry. Our instructor, Mac Hassler, guided us with formal and informal writing prompts, and he also taught us how to keep a regular journal and then to incorporate our journaling into finished poems that could have a shape and voice all their own. This pedagogy is a foundation for the creative writing courses I teach now at Columbia College Chicago. Back then, it was a revelation that the four walls of the classroom could be an environment for intimate life-writing.

Poetry, then, came to me foremost as a personal thing: an art form that documents our emotions as they collide with the outside world. Poetry revealed itself as the artistic practice best suited for exploring the mysterious emotional narrative arc of my life. I was drawn to poetry because it gives me access to the vulnerable, the strange, the unsayable in what otherwise seems ordinary.

A poem is a document of an ordinary person making discoveries about the self and the world while passing through a brief moment in time. This spirit is at the core of a documentary collection like my book *Proof Something Happened*, and it's also crucial to my autobiographical work. In an immediate, ongoing way, this aesthetic serves as the conceptual blueprint for my multivolume experiment in poetic memoir, *The Complete* Dark Shadows *(of My Childhood)*, published by BlazeVOX [books]. As part of my research for this series of books, I'm re-watching every episode of the old 1960s gothic soap opera, *Dark Shadows*, which I saw every afternoon with my mother when I was a small child. Back then, sitting in front of the television with her on the sagging, gray couch in our living room, I became obsessed with the show's main character, a two-centuries-old vampire named Barnabas Collins. I was afflicted with constant nightmares about him, and I went so far as to hunch my shoulders at night, thinking this would prevent him from biting my neck when I slept. (Evidently, it worked: when I checked the mirror every morning, I was relieved to find no vampire puncture wounds.) For this project, I write one sentence in response to each *Dark Shadows* episode, then shape these sentences into poetry, prose, and hybrid forms, using each sentence as a trigger for autobiographical explorations.

The most recent book, *Ghosts of the Upper Floor*, the third install-ment in the series, was published in 2019. I'm in the process of draft-ing Book 4. The show ran for 1,225 episodes, which means I'll need several more volumes to finish the project. Proust had his madeleine; I have my vampire.

It's difficult, but necessary, to pay attention closely enough to make art that documents an ordinary life, whether I'm rendering my life or that of a person in a documentary poetry collection. See-ing clearly, casting my vision both wide and deep, requires conscious effort. Ever since childhood, I've turned to poetry to imagine a lan-guage for vision. I want to read and write poems that teach me to see. "The eye altering," as William Blake writes, "alters all."

CHAPTER ONE

Obstinance as a Poetics

It was 2008, and I'd just finished reading from my first book of poems, *The Lama's English Lessons*, at Schlafly Bottleworks in St. Louis. I stood with my back pressed against the bar as the next reader took the stage. A member of the audience, a young man who looked to be in his early twenties, walked over.

He said he enjoyed my poems. Then he asked, "What advice do you have for a writer who's just starting out?"

I'd been teaching undergraduate and graduate student poets at Columbia College Chicago for nearly ten years already. I was comfortable in my professorial identity. Dispensing writing advice is an integral part of the job. But right then, as I leaned against a bar in St. Louis, I found myself trying to offer guidance to a younger writer outside the four walls of the classroom, beyond the comfortable boundaries of the fifteen-week semester and the three-hour class session, far removed from curriculum plans and assigned texts. I feared that if I said the wrong thing, I might derail his fledgling writing career. This feeling that I had the power to disrupt another writer's career trajectory was a result of bravado on my part. At the time, I worried that my first book of poems might either be panned or, worse, ignored. Deep down, I wasn't confident I could offer any meaningful reply to his question.

I had only a few minutes to respond before the next reader began. She was situating herself at the microphone and I didn't want to be rude, hold a conversation with someone else while she was reading.

"Be stubborn," I blurted out. The words came to me spontaneously. I'd never before encouraged a student to consider obstinance as a poetics.

My father was the most obstinate man I'd ever met. I loved him immensely, yet his stubbornness strained his relationship with my mother and, at times, with my siblings and me. Even so, I unconsciously absorbed his obstinance into my own personality, which, no surprise, sometimes made it difficult for me to sustain friendships and relationships. I had driven alone to St. Louis for the reading. I didn't realize it yet, but my first marriage was on the verge of ending, and my stubborn personality played no small role in the breakup.

Still, I repeated, "You really just have to be stubborn."

He looked at me strangely, as if disappointed that I hadn't talked about, for instance, my writing process or my strategy for submitting work to journals and presses. I realized I should say more, and that I had to do it quickly so that I could hear the next reader.

"You need to have a belief in the power of your imagination, faith in your creative process that runs so deep that you're too stubborn to give up."

"That's all? You have to believe you're a good writer. That's it."

I nodded.

"But everyone feels this way."

"You don't want to believe in your work when it's no good," I added, leaning forward, lowering my voice as the writer on stage thanked the reading series curators and the brewery. I could feel a soliloquy coming on. A friend of mine once said the reason Nathaniel Hawthorne is one of my favorite writers is that, like him, I talk in paragraphs.

I tried to be brief so that we could both hear the next reader.

"You want to believe in yourself so much that when obstacles get in the way, like rejections from editors, you can stubbornly persist. You don't want to be so obstinate that you ignore editors when they say a piece of writing isn't ready to be published. By 'stubborn,' I mean that you believe in yourself so much that when you get rejection after rejection after rejection, which happens to every writer, you don't lose your commitment to making your writing better."

He took a step backward. He was either considering the merits of what I was saying or he had decided to just put distance between us and end the conversation. "Stubbornness" was not what I'd expected to say, nor, it seemed, was it within the realm of writerly advice he'd expected to hear.

"It's hard enough being an artist in a utilitarian culture that doesn't value what we make or do," I added. "You don't want to make things worse by allowing the outside world to destroy your belief that your imaginative labor can make you a better writer."

Another awkward pause. Then he asked me to sign his copy of the book.

.

I kept thinking about this conversation during the five-hour drive back to Chicago the next day. I couldn't figure out why I reached for "stubbornness" in response to this audience member who clearly had put forth the kind of fundamental question that is a typical feature of question-and-answer sessions at the end of readings. In such situations, you're usually asked about how to submit poems or essays to literary journals, how to put together a full manuscript and where to send manuscripts, how to find the discipline required to complete a full-length book, and so on—all manner of pragmatic, nuts-and-bolts questions that emerging writers want answered. Looking back now, one of the reasons I went straight for the more esoteric answer was, simply, that I'm not convinced that good writing advice can emerge from the kind of one-size-fits-all environment of a post-reading question-and-answer session. I was still relatively new to the publishing world, and my concern that night in St. Louis was for the poems from my new book to connect with an audience. But even then, I was suspicious of the expectation I'd seen so often from my fellow audience members at readings that if you asked the right question, in the right way, the writer would deliver a bullet-point list of how-to advice that, like a magic spell, would launch your writing career. In hindsight, I don't think the person who asked me "What advice do you have for a writer who's just starting out?" was looking for an easy fix. But I felt this way back then—and, worse, I didn't believe I had quite enough experience yet to give him a satisfying answer.

Instead of taking a pragmatic approach to his query, I responded with something orphic, as if I were pointing to the word "stubborn" in the middle of a poem and asking him to hold the word up to the light and turn it in multiple angles of vision to see just how many refracted meanings he could come up with. I wondered if his hesitance, his long pause before asking me to sign the book, was an indication that I had disappointed him. I truly wanted to answer his question, but my altruistic intent was far removed from what became its confusing impact. At the same time, I felt—and still do—that I gave him a valuable answer.

I still believed in my response, in the value of writerly stubbornness, but as I drove home I tried to figure out why stubbornness had been so squarely on my mind the previous evening after the reading.

I remembered something one of my percussion teachers, Dave Robinson, said to me back in my early twenties. Dave was the drummer for The Numbers Band, an avant-blues group with an enormous Midwest following. They were the house band at JBs, in Kent, Ohio, where I was an undergraduate student at Kent State University. Dave and I were discussing a particularly complicated, alternating-accent triplet beat that had taken weeks for me to master. For this lesson, I proudly showed off a modified version of the beat—a simpler, stripped-down variation that fit a new song that my band, Incline, was working on. I played my version for him then scanned his face for the wry, crooked smile that always told me I had impressed my teacher.

"What you played works fine," he said eventually. "It's steady and it has a dynamic pattern. Good variation. But it doesn't sing like the original version we've been working on."

I straightened myself in the chair. I'd expected unconditional approval and was surprised that I felt the need to defend myself.

"I like how my version fits the song we're writing. It comes off a little less pretentious than the original beat you played for me. Like you always say, I don't want to just show off my chops on stage."

At that time in my life, what held me back the most as a musician was that I wanted nothing more than to demonstrate virtuosity on stage, even if this came at the expense of the songs themselves. Dave, as my drum teacher, knew this better than anyone.

"But when you really think about it, nothing's more pretentious than assuming other people want to come to a club and pay a cover charge to hear you play music," he said. "We all need to feel 'pretentious' just to get on stage at all. Just to assume an audience cares enough to want to see you play. Even when you're having a bad day, you have to go into a show with the total expectation that you're talented enough for people to think they're going to have a good time watching you perform."

He was right, of course. As I recalled Dave's remarks on my drive home from St. Louis, I realized the extent to which I'd absorbed his peculiar—but useful—redefinition of "pretentious." We're often taught that pretension is a character flaw, the result of an overweening and unearned belief in one's talent and importance. But Dave helped me see a flip side to pretension. In his reformulation, the word felt more like an honorable form of audacity. How audacious to think that an audience wanted to go to a club and pay to see my band perform songs we'd written and rehearsed in our moldy basement studio. But without such audacity, it would be too easy to surrender to the fear that I might fail, that an audience would leave one of our shows regretting they'd come in the first place. Wasn't stubbornness, then, a variation of the pretension and audacity that allows you to believe you have something to say—and believe other people want to hear it?

Stubbornness is a complicated personality trait, especially for someone like myself who grew up watching my father's stubbornness alienate his family. Stubbornness can quell the fear that we have nothing to say, but it also can be a manifestation of insecurity. When I doubt myself, I tend to talk over, or ignore, the opposing viewpoints of others. Digging in my heels is often about uncertainty and wanting to (stubbornly) control a situation that could become chaotic. As vital as it is to believe in yourself, an inflated self-regard can be nothing but narcissism.

But even though pretension and stubbornness can be nothing but bluster, they also can provide the extra spark of confidence to propel you to make art. If not for a stubborn belief in the importance of your work, you might never leave that moldy basement studio and perform. Art is, at its core, a mode of communication with others, and sometimes it's only stubbornness and pretension that allow us to share our work with an audience—that prevent us from talking only to ourselves.

·

What I said in St. Louis that night in 2008 came out of nowhere, it seemed. I was asked for advice on how to write, and instead of talking about practicalities, I blurted out something about stubbornness. But I don't mean to suggest that "stubbornness" just came to me out of nowhere, a lightning bolt of inspiration while leaning against the bar. Instead, this kind of insight often comes through friction, in moments when you're forced to account for a viewpoint that goes against normative standards of behavior, when you realize that what seems organic and natural to you might be perceived as unnatural by others.

This happens enough and you either capitulate, or you find a vocabulary to dig yourself out and come up with a perspective that doesn't judge your life practice as unnatural.

A couple decades before the St. Louis reading, on a summer afternoon in 1985, I stood in front of the desk of my academic advisor in the Kent State School of Journalism, a crusty, old-school, chain-smoking journalist named Bruce Larrick. I was a promising student. Bruce was my mentor, and he'd already invested a lot of energy in my development as a journalist. The previous year, I'd won the *Daily Kent Stater* Outstanding Freshman Staff Writer Award, and just a couple months earlier, I'd won the *Stater*'s annual award as the paper's best sportswriter. I was nineteen, the youngest Sports Editor in the history of the paper. But journalistic writing wasn't imaginative enough for me. Writing against a daily deadline helped me develop focused and disciplined work habits, but the writing itself felt stale and formulaic. With the exception of long-form investigative reporting, most journalistic writing came off as predictable to me, like when you're talking to someone whose ideas are so familiar that you have to fight yourself not to interrupt and finish their sentences for them.

Somehow, I'd found the guts—or Bruce might've called it "gall"— to make an office-hour appointment to tell him that I was changing my major, leaving behind a promising career in Journalism to study English. I was intimidated by Bruce, as almost all the Journalism School students were.

Standing in front of his desk, I watched him pull hard on his Marlboro as he considered what to say.

"What the hell are you doing that for?" Bruce said finally.

He stubbed out the cigarette.

"I don't want to spend the rest of my life trying to figure out how to make Akron City Council meetings sound exciting."

I took a step back, hands in my pockets. I went into journalism because I wanted to be Woodward and Bernstein. I watched *All the*

President's Men five or six times my senior year of high school.

"Why the fuck are you going to major in English? You know that English teachers are a dime a dozen."

"And journalists aren't?"

Looking back, I can't believe I had the courage to insult the profession of this stocky, hard-bitten journalist who looked like he was on the verge of slugging me.

I remembered *Stater* editor Jeff McVann telling me about a job interview he'd just aced at a newspaper in Florida.

"The last thing they asked me was whether I see myself as a 'writer' or a 'reporter.' Interviewers ask this all the time. You have to say 'reporter' or you won't get the job. As far as they're concerned, you write your novel on your own time," Jeff said.

I had assumed the correct answer was "writer."

Bruce pulled out another cigarette.

"You can't just write when inspiration hits you. It doesn't work like that. You've seen it, working on a daily paper. You gotta meet the four-p.m. deadline every day, no exceptions. You fuck up your deadline, you fuck with everyone else's, too. You can't just smoke a joint every night after work and expect lightning to strike so you can write the Great American Novel."

He turned his head and blew smoke out his window.

"I tried that," he added. "It doesn't work."

I wanted to tell him that I had no intention of writing a novel. I was a poet and a musician. If I failed as a writer, my dream was to play drums with Black Flag. I could never be happy pretending that a story about a contentious city council meeting would be as satisfying as breaking the news of Richard Nixon's Saturday Night Massacre.

"I'll never lose the discipline I've learned in J-School." I said. "But I have to believe I have something in me that goes beyond newswriting. I want to use the word 'very' if I think it's necessary. I want to write paragraphs that are longer than one sentence. I can't be someone who only covers other people's lectures and performances. I want to do my own. I'm not finished with being on stage."

I don't know how I summoned the courage to face down Bruce like that. No one defied him this way. What's more, I barely believed in my own writing at the time. I was sending poems to journals and they were all coming back rejected. Still, I had faith I could make a writing practice for myself that could stay with me, and be refined, for my entire life. I didn't realize (yet) that art-making could be a career—I was a first-generation college student from a poor family, and I had no role models for a life in art—but I knew I had the potential to create a life practice out of writing. I just had to stubbornly believe that I had the discipline to do it, and that if I developed a single-minded focus, one day I actually would compose poems and essays that other people wanted to read.

I went home, got high and listened to Black Flag's newest album, *Slip It In*. I was still a long way from creating a consistent writing practice. I had no idea how much work it would take over the years to become a writer who actually had an audience. But at some unconscious level, beyond what I could describe, I knew I made the right decision to leave journalism and become a writer. It felt like the only choice I could make—writing, rather than reporting.

.

I couldn't have mustered the strength to face Bruce that day without the prior experience of standing up to my father's utilitarianism with a belief in my own potential as an artist. As a child, I coped with my parents' constant bickering by going to my room, shutting my door, and drawing comics while listening to music. I couldn't do anything else. Couldn't stand being in the same room when they argued. And they didn't want me there anyway. Like most couples, their fighting resembled a pitched courtroom battle, and if you were not a judge, juror, attorney, or star witness, you simply weren't needed in court. In childhood, I nurtured an obstinate practice: while my parents fought, I could make my own worlds of pleasure and delight with my door closed and my sketchpad and notebook in front of me.

My father grew up during the Great Depression, and his stubbornness was a survival trait he learned in a first-generation immigrant family that required an obstinacy of their own to survive in a land so far away from "the old country," as they called Italy. My own stubbornness would also become a source of strength, just as much a character trait as it was a defense mechanism. I needed to be able to stand up to my father when he tried to convince me not to pursue art-making as a way of life. Keep away from art: strange advice from a man who, despite the deprivations of his Depression-era childhood, came from a family of musicians. His own father was on tour with a jazz band when he was born. When I was eight, he encouraged me to take guitar lessons from my Uncle Rich. These failed when I realized my fingers were too short and chubby to make proper chords. A few years later, I took drum lessons from my cousin Jim (son of the uncle who tried to teach me guitar) and I was so successful that my father encouraged me to keep playing. Music—this was comprehensible to him. You could make extra money playing at bars and weddings on weekends. But back then, as much as I loved the drums—an instrument I still play now, a few records and a tour later—I really just wanted to be a comic book artist.

Which is exactly what I told him one day, 1976, age ten. I'd discovered a nearby summer art program in rural, upstate New York that I was sure would help me hone my craft. I was worried that no matter what it cost, it would be too expensive for him. We were always a couple missed paychecks from being put on the street, as he often reminded my mother and me. But, stubborn as I was, I asked him to sign me up for the program anyway.

"Artists are born, not made," he said, waving his hand, sweeping away my question.

I pretended I believed him. "I know. That's why I want to go to art school." I considered myself a born artist who wanted to find a teacher who could make me better.

He eventually relented. Yes, we couldn't afford the summer art program. But he told me about a correspondence course, Cartoonists Exchange, that one of his coworkers at the steel factory had taken. It hadn't occurred to me to ask if the coworker was now making comics. But what mattered most of all was that by being stubborn—by not surrendering to the debilitating axiom, "artists are born, not made"—I had persuaded my father to give me an opportunity to learn visual art.

Writers are both born *and* made. You're born with some kind of linguistic talent, but, like any muscle you don't use, it can atrophy unless you study and practice the craft—unless you take what you've been born with and make something out of it. But in a culture that often is suspicious of the urge to make art, and that seems to distrust the urgency of art, you have to be pretty damn stubborn and persistent to make it work. Not only will you, as a writer, face enough editorial rejection to scatter calluses all over your psyche, you'll also risk being dismissed by people (even family members) who are intimidated by your audacious conviction that you can succeed as a writer. We all have to be stubborn to push through this resistance. Sometimes you must possess a pretentious belief in your own talent just to walk on stage in the first place. If you can stubbornly hold on to this "firm persuasion," as William Blake would call it, then you have a better chance of cultivating the stamina to nurture an artistic career through the inevitable psychological storms produced by rejection.

Still, my firm persuasion aside, I feel compelled to emphasize, again (with a healthy dose of obstinance), that even though I believe stubbornness should be taken seriously as an element of a writer's craft, I don't want to suggest that we become rigidly defensive when others point out where our work needs to improve. That's not stubborn. It's thick-headed and self-sabotaging. Instead, this book begins by encouraging you to be stubborn enough to believe that you can create the kind of discipline for steady, sustained writing. With a consistent writing practice—daily or weekly, whatever your schedule allows—and persistent, imaginative labor, your work will develop into individual pieces that can be shaped into books that other people will want to read.

At times I'll talk about the kinds of subject matter traditionally found in dictionaries of craft and technique. I'll be sharing stories informed by conventional matters of poetic form and content, such as language, voice, persona, and poetic form, for example. But as I talk about my development as a writer, I'll also emphasize sources of inspiration not usually found in craft handbooks—blogging, psychic channeling, documentary writing, arcana, and meditation, among others. Whether discussing traditional or unconventional craft elements, each chapter proceeds from a common belief that the most effective way to learn one's own craft is through storytelling, rather than the linear, business-memo pragmatism of how-to handbooks. My hope is that you will recognize your own desires as a writer in these stories, and that they will inspire you to create your own work and, audaciously, share this work with an audience.

CHAPTER TWO

How Do Short Pieces of Writing Become Full-Length Books?

I first heard the word "craft" in graduate school. Craft-based discussion was a common, unifying feature in all of my creative writing workshops. We experimented with craft elements as we generated new poetry and prose, and our understanding of craft provided an anchor for our weekly workshop critiques. Classroom craft discussions sparked some of my most important ideas about how to revise my writing and produce new work. Studying craft and technique helped me understand the strengths and weaknesses of the writing I brought to my poetry workshops, and inspired me to stretch myself and take risks in the new poems I was working on.

The classroom was a laboratory for craft. Still, our experiments in this laboratory could only reach their potential if we were also writing and revising outside of class. The work habits of my graduate school roommate Mitch Evich demonstrated what a steady, diligent writing routine could look like beyond the four walls of the classroom. Inspired by Mitch's example, I created such a practice for myself, one that I've nurtured and sustained in the years since graduate school. Mitch and I lived from 1989–91 in a third-floor apartment of a triple-decker house on Lowell Street in Somerville, Massachusetts, just outside Boston. He was finishing his first novel, *The Destiny of Salmon*, based on his high school and college experiences working on a fishing boat in the Pacific Northwest. Mitch was the first writer I'd met who could turn nearly every literary conversation into a discussion of craft. We spent many late nights in our kitchen and living room talking about how to apply to our own work the key craft elements— language and structure, narrative and voice, character and persona, among others—that were foundational to our favorite poems, stories, and novels. Our conversations almost always circled back to how, as the poet Robert Creeley described it, form and content could be extensions of each other in a piece of writing.

Watching Mitch summon the discipline to write nearly every day and finish his novel taught me that I needed to be a much more organized writer than I was. I needed to start planning and scheduling my available writing time so that, like Mitch, my writing sessions could be steadier and more productive than my current writing habits were. I wanted to find a way to write with more regularity, whether I wrote every day or just once or twice per week. Mitch's understanding that a writing session had to be intentionally planned, along with his discipline in keeping to his writing schedule, were craft elements just as important as the technical questions of form and content that we constantly talked about.

He knew that he couldn't rely on random lightning strikes of inspiration if he was going to finish the novel. Mitch sat every day at his computer as if his bedroom writing space were an office cubicle. I don't mean to suggest that writing was a form of nine-to-five drudgery for him. From our seemingly endless craft discussions, it was obvious to me that he saw writing as a form of play. But, significantly, he also felt that you had to treat the writing process like a workaday job so that it actually could be playful. After all, if you're not producing steady, sustained writing, then you won't have much material to play with in the first place. Seeing him sit at his desk almost every day, adding to his novel word-by-word and page-by-page with no guarantee that an agent or publisher would be waiting for it on the other side, taught me that, with persistence, short pieces of writing can accumulate into longer, book-length work.

I reread *The Destiny of Salmon* in the spring of 2021, as I emerged from the dark February of Chicago's COVID-19 lockdown. I recalled the profound influence I felt three decades earlier, when I lived in Somerville with Mitch and watched him write the novel in short bursts day after day. Back then I knew, theoretically, that writing a book required discipline and intentionality. Every craft handbook I read in graduate school, and every creative writing professor I studied with, emphasized that, contrary to stereotype, we can't depend on spontaneous lightning strikes of inspiration if we aspire to a career as a writer. Looking back now, it seems to me that unless you've already cultivated a steady writing practice, you might not even notice the lightning crack in the sky—and the electrical charge we call "inspiration"—when it actually does happen. But as a graduate student, I hadn't yet realized that consistently writing day after day could be more conducive to inspiration than waiting to be jolted by an external muse.

Sharing an apartment with Mitch while he wrote the novel allowed me to witness this kind of consistency firsthand. It changed me irrevocably as a writer. I was an ambitious poet, but my writing practice had been disorganized and chaotic. I'd heard lots of writers explain in interviews and lectures that the only way they could finish a project was to write nearly every day. *Write nearly every day* is sound advice. A book doesn't materialize all at once. Instead, it's the product of persistent writing—if not every day, then at least often and consistent enough that you can apply sustained attention to the writing at hand, nurturing and shaping the work over time into a full manuscript. But for the longest time, I didn't know what it looked like to write nearly every day. I couldn't conceive of such an artistic practice. As an unorganized person in my twenties with an attention span that ran wild, I found it almost impossible to sit in a chair for hours at a time and write. I was content to collect scraps of language whenever I could, usually while reading books by other poets, and then haphazardly stitch these scraps into poem drafts. I tried to use my free time wisely to write; but until I watched Mitch compose his novel, I didn't know how to schedule regular writing time and stick to it. I'd never seen anyone actually write this way.

·

Several years ago, my college brought the acclaimed poet Terrance Hayes to campus for a reading. During the question-and-answer session afterward, one of our students described for Hayes her difficulty in constructing a steady, consistent writing schedule for herself.

"Writers always say you have to write every day. But do people actually do this?" she asked.

I recognized my younger self in her question. I remembered how difficult it was back in graduate school to reconcile my drive to be a writer with the fact that I simply didn't know how to make the writing process a steady, habitual part of my life. Her question recalled all the times I attended readings as a student and wanted to hear a visiting writer take us through the pragmatic nuts-and-bolts details of their artistic practice. I never raised my hand and asked about this—insecurity and shyness on my part, afraid it was a question everyone else but me knew the answer to.

"I do try to write almost every day," Hayes said. "I want to carve out enough time, maybe two or three hours at a sitting, to pay the kind of attention that the poems need."

Then he paused and backed away slightly from the podium.

"Actually," he continued, leaning back toward the microphone, "when I say I write for two or three hours at a time, what I really mean is that I might play video games for the first half hour or an hour, just to loosen up, then I'll write for the next couple hours. I don't know many writers who can sit down at the computer and write for three hours straight."

It's still the best writing advice I've heard in my three decades of attending readings and hearing audience members ask about a writer's work habits. Hayes described for the student a consistent writing schedule that is deliberately planned and organized. His reply depicted a schedule so attentive to the needs of the artistic imagination that it even included space for random, non-textual play.

Back when I lived with Mitch, I was so prone to distraction that it was a revelation just to see someone, especially a roommate and friend, sit in front of his computer for three hours at a stretch (in Mitch's case, sometimes four or five) and write. I had never seen anyone schedule their art-making time with such regularity, writing nearly every day with the confidence that these individual sessions in front of the computer would yield short pieces of writing that could be developed over weeks and months into a book. I don't know if his writing schedule allowed time for video games, but he did take frequent breaks to read the day's edition of the *Boston Globe* sports section. He seemed to be giving his mind the permission to wander as far away from the novel as he could, with the confidence that he'd return fresh and energized from those playful forays in the *Globe* sports pages.

He always set weekly word-count goals for himself, too, as a way of keeping his individual writing sessions as focused and productive as possible, even when the inevitable fatigue would set in. I do the same to this day when I'm writing prose. The first draft of this book was completed under the guidance of a self-imposed, one-thousand-words-per-week writing schedule. Word-count goals allow me to decide when I can stop writing and take the rest of the day off to allow my imagination to cool down. I remember the many times I saw Mitch leave his room after a writing session and amble into the kitchen to make dinner for himself. He looked relaxed, satisfied that he'd accomplished something. Even if that day's writing later proved to be flat and would need extensive revision, he still could make dinner in that particular moment and allow his imagination to take a break from the novel. Often, he cooked salmon, its stench saturating the kitchen, an odor I'd smell long into the night because the door to my bedroom was just a few feet from the oven. I don't eat fish, but to this day I associate the smell of salmon with the discipline required to write a book.

·

Individual pieces of writing grow into manuscripts through regular sessions of writing and revising. But the blunt reality is that few of us, myself included, can write for a few hours each day and balance all the other necessary demands of everyday life. Other people depend on us—our biological families, our chosen families, our friends, our neighbors—and if we want to live a full life, we can't neglect them for our writing. Nor can we neglect our jobs, since our employers are, for most of us, our primary means of financial support and health insurance.

Rather than trying to force the writing time into a schedule that might not be able to accommodate it, I try to adapt the needs of my writing to the rhythms of my work life and personal life. All I ask of myself is that I maintain a continuity in my writing practice so that the shorter pieces I'm working on can develop, at the pace they need, into a larger whole. It doesn't matter whether this continuity unfolds daily, every other day, once per week, or every couple weeks. I can't just write once in a while, waiting for the optimal environment of solitude and quiet to present itself. Inconsistency makes it difficult for me to create a sustained, long-term relationship with my writing. When I go long periods without working on a project, I feel like I have to start everything from scratch when I return to it—like reconnecting with an old friend I haven't seen in years and spending the entire visit getting to know each other all over again. If I don't consciously schedule steady, regular time to write, then I risk losing the intimate connections I've nurtured with the sound and rhythm of my words, with my characters and personas, and most of all with the discovery process itself. And if I'm not discovering something new as I write, then it's almost certain that my readers won't, either.

My wife Liz is also a teacher and writer, and we both know how difficult it is to set aside time to write. But we find a way. Given the pressures of our teaching commitments, if we're going to write, we have to schedule it. We don't have a choice, if we want to have a life, too. My weeks at Columbia College Chicago are filled with curriculum planning, grading, committee meetings, and office-hour conferences, in addition to teaching and directing graduate theses, and I have to be intentional about finding time to write. During the academic year, neither Liz nor I can maintain a daily writing practice. If we did, we'd have little time for each other, let alone for the other people in our lives who depend on us, and whom we depend on. But we find ways to schedule two or three writing sessions per week. We squeeze them in between classes when we can, or schedule writing time early in the morning, late at night, or on weekend afternoons. We're both active on the major social media platforms, but we don't post so much that it saps the energy for our own writing. (Back in the early days of social media, I was so addicted to Facebook that I actually had to add a software app, LeechBlock, that would kick me off the site if I spent more than fifteen minutes at a time on it.) We don't neglect our personal or teaching obligations, but we schedule the time in our weekly planners so that each writing session is as important as anything else we log in our schedules—social events, family gatherings, religious holidays, doctor's appointments, and so on. How many times per week we write is less important for us than making sure we are writing something each week. The regularity of the writing allows us the time to make discoveries as we write, to approach the drafting and revision process with the patience needed to recognize what we're trying to say in our work.

.

Mitch died in 2021. For almost a decade, he suffered from early-onset Alzheimer's disease, first diagnosed when he was fifty-three. He kept a steady writing practice as long as he could, chronicling his life with the disease in a blog, *The Diminishing Window*, which he kept from 2015 until 2019, when Alzheimer's eventually made it too difficult for him to continue. I'm still haunted by his blog posting from March 4, 2016, describing the existential dread of knowing that the disease was getting worse, and that, no matter how much research the medical community was devoting to its eradication, he wouldn't live long enough to see a cure.

"Will I still be *me*," he wrote in that blog posting, "my sense of self intact, however circumscribed, when plaques and tangles have colonized my brain?"

I'd visited him earlier that month and noticed how often he got lost in the middle of sentences, completely pulled away, it seemed, into an inaccessible desert island of the mind. It was crushing to see the baffled isolation in his eyes, my dear friend of three decades, when Alzheimer's whisked him away from a conversation. By 2020, he essentially couldn't speak at all, couldn't form enough words to make a complete sentence during our pandemic telephone and Zoom calls. We no longer could exchange long, filibuster-like soliloquies about craft. Mitch's crisp, precise words were gone. Yet somehow, with a mutual, dogged persistence, we created brief patches of lucidity amid the fog.

I never actually considered that our constant craft talks would end, even after he first told me about his diagnosis (total denial on my part). But Alzheimer's is sadistic, and it eventually robbed him of speech. The disease disrupted his vision so badly that, in his final days, he no longer could read. This symptom didn't manifest until a couple weeks before he was admitted into hospice, and it was a small mercy to know that he was able to do something he loved so much, read fiction and poetry, up until the end. He died on Christmas Day 2021. His wife Paula emailed on Christmas Eve to let me know Mitch had been moved to the hospice wing of the North Reading, Massachusetts, nursing home where he was admitted the day before Thanksgiving. I called a few minutes later. Paula put the phone by his ear and I said goodbye. Mitch replied with a grunt, a guttural farewell from a writer who used to speak in enormous paragraphs, a tendency I share. Later that day, I texted the news to another close friend, Kevin Cassell, who lives in Arizona. We grieved together over a long text-message exchange, and I spent most of it talking about the final phone call. "That's beautiful how one grunt can make your whole day," Kevin wrote, "in fact, your whole month if not your whole year."

CHAPTER THREE

Performance Journaling

One of the most effective ways to develop a sustained writing practice is to keep a regular journal or notebook. Journaling can provide a generative space for consistent, uninhibited writing. We tend to see a writing journal or notebook as a private space for work that later can be shaped into polished writing for a public audience. But taking one's journal or notebook public can sometimes exert an even greater effect on our writing. I'd maintained a writer's notebook for years without ever thinking that the private act of journaling could be public and performative. This relationship between journaling and performance—and the effect the two had on my own writing—only became apparent once I grew tired, finally, of apologizing for my lovely but deranged cat, Shimmy.

In 1996, when my first wife Shelly and I lived in Boston, Shimmy attacked Mitch's two-year-old son, Andryc. Shelly and I adopted Shimmy in 1994 after a colleague found her abandoned, near death, in the wooded suburbs of Boston's south shore. The veterinarian who saved her life estimated that she had survived on her own, somehow, for three or four weeks—a period that left a feral mark upon her, as we would soon learn. Two years later, on a cold, midwinter Sunday morning, Mitch and Andryc came to visit. Andryc had never met Shimmy. She was a paranoid cat, suspicious of most visitors, but we didn't think she would pose a danger. Her response to strangers was usually a quick, ferocious hiss before she fled under the living room couch. Her reaction to Mitch and Andryc's visit that afternoon demonstrated just how much psychological damage her period of kitten-abandonment had inflicted upon her. Their visit was yet another reminder that the feral aggression Shimmy needed to survive as a castaway in the sub-urban forest was a dominant force in her personality—one that might not easily, if ever, go away.

Andryc yelled, "Kitty!" as soon as he stumbled through the door, likely enthralled that Shimmy resembled his own cat. He rushed from our foyer to the living room to pet her. Shimmy ran away, galloping toward her favorite hiding spot beneath the living room couch. It was a reasonable reaction under the circumstances for any small creature concerned with self-preservation in the presence of an excited child determined to physically embrace them.

But then, for some reason, Shimmy stopped abruptly, turning in mid-flight, as if suddenly remembering this was her turf and she needed to stand her ground against Andryc, who was, for her, noth-ing more than a predatory intruder.

Shimmy remained still, frozen in battle posture before the couch. She glared at Andryc, her back fur spiked and standing on end. I'd seen her respond this way to visitors many times before, but it always ended with her hiding underneath the couch.

Andryc advanced toward her, arms outstretched, gleefully un-aware that our cat was tracing his every micro-gesture, ready to strike if he got too close.

Shimmy took a cautious, warlike step forward.

She reared on her haunches and wound up her right arm, claws fully extended, like she was wielding a medieval mace.

I tried to get between the two of them. I wasn't quick enough. It all happened too fast for anyone to stop it, yet my memory replays the incident in slow-motion, Shimmy's arm flashing in what seemed like half-speed as she attacked the two-year-old boy running toward her. But looking back now, I see her swinging with a whip-crack flash, her pumpkin-colored fur leaving blurry, cartoon motion trails behind it, striking Andryc's arm, her translucent claws sinking as far as they could go into the blue vinyl and puffy goose-lining of his winter jacket.

I grabbed Shimmy and moved her a safe distance from Andryc. She hissed at him—a final, defiant spit.

We were lucky Andryc wore a thick jacket that day; Shimmy's claws did nothing but puncture the lining. But as I said later to Mitch, I feared our cat had caused a primal trauma that would haunt his son into adulthood. (Many years later, twenty-four-year-old Andryc nonchalantly told me he didn't remember a thing about the incident. I'm not sure he even believed me when I narrated the details.)

Once the situation calmed down—after Andryc screamed himself hoarse, in heaving sobs, to his mother Paula on the telephone, and I had apologized over and over—it occurred to me that for most of her life I had been apologizing for Shimmy.

"I don't know what to do sometimes," I said to Mitch. "It's like having a child who's an arsonist. You love her with all your heart, but you keep saying things to your neighbors like, 'I'm sorry Shimmy burned down your tool shed. We'll pay all the damages.'"

This would be my operative apology over the years: *I'm sorry, she's unhinged but we love her.* We wanted to help her abide calmly in what she seemed to believe was a perpetually hostile world, but we couldn't deny the trouble she caused. We did everything we could to provide a safe, predictable domestic life for her, but of course, she was a cat after all, not a child, and we knew she'd never domesticate completely—especially with her early kitten memories of starving in the woods in late-summer 1994 before we adopted her.

Every action she undertook was uncensored, and Shelly and I came to admire over the years this untamable feral instinct, a rage that was crucial to her survival those first few weeks of her life when she got lost from (or was abandoned by) her mother. Shimmy's child-arsonist persona was a reminder of what lies unfettered inside us, combining that which can be loved like an adorable child with a demon-spawn threat as terrifying as the glow-eyed children from the classic 1960 film *Village of the Damned* (and its equally scary 1964 sequel, *Children of the Damned*).

Our move from Boston to Chicago in 1998, two years after Shimmy attacked Andryc, only made things worse. She hid under the bed for six weeks, no matter how gently we tried to entice her out with her favorite food, Chicken of the Sea Tuna.

I found myself writing about her more and more as part of my regular correspondence with friends. In long letters about new writing projects, or about my often buffoonish efforts to navigate a new city that felt hundreds of times larger than Boston, I'd find myself returning again and again to anthropomorphic descriptions of Shimmy's own struggle to adapt to our new home. Sometimes I even spoke in her voice at the end of letters. I knew I was treading on dangerous ground, talking in the voice of my cat. I had to trust, as my letter-writing friends did, that I never would become someone who bought cat calendars and sent "Hang in There" stock photographs of kittens hanging by their front paws on a clothesline.

As I increasingly added material in Shimmy's voice to my emails and letters, I began to notice opportunities for Shimmy's untamed opinions and feelings to find their way into poems I was writing. I added a Shimmy-postscript once in an email to my cousin Michael Trigilio in a letter full of foaming-at-the-mouth vitriol about Kenneth Starr (the zealous prosecutor in President Bill Clinton's 1999 impeachment trial) that later would provide material for my poem, "Special Prosecutor," in *The Lama's English Lessons*. This postscript anticipated Shimmy's imaginary encounter in 2006 with former United States Secretary of Defense Donald Rumsfeld (as I'll discuss later in this chapter). "Shimmy is upset because neither you nor anyone else we know rescued her from her vet checkup at the Den of Spies last week," I wrote in the postscript to Michael. As I channeled Shimmy's feral-cat rage against the world, she revealed to me in this email that her secret name for the veterinarian's office was the "Den of Spies," the name that Islamist radicals bestowed on the U.S. embassy in Iran when they attacked it in 1979. According to Shimmy, her veterinarian was not Dr. Bow, a caring doctor with the patience of a saint for treating our raving cat, but instead was Dr. Henry Kissinger, the former U.S. Secretary of State who, in Shimmy's mind, strutted around the Uptown Animal Hospital in a blood-stained butcher's apron.

"Dr. Kissinger touched me all over, Michael," Shimmy wrote, "and you should have heard the rustic hacking of those mangy dogs—I wanted to strangle them with my bare hands." Nothing particularly poetic or even eloquent. The plea to my cousin in the voice of my cat instead was simply a raw, uncensored burst of prose like any other I might compose in a first draft, taking it or leaving it, not worried about judging it as "good" or "bad" writing.

Around this time, as Shimmy spoke in the postscripts to my letters, and my friends responded back to both Shimmy and me (humoring me? humoring themselves?), I discovered poets' blogs. I was intrigued that blogs could function as public versions of private journals. I assumed that poets' blogs would reveal the secret minute particulars of their creative processes—that blogs would reveal hidden crawlspaces in the finished architecture of contemporary poems. To an extent this was true, and the best example was Ron Silliman's brilliant (though dogmatic) near-daily blog postings on contemporary poetics. Sadly, though, most poets' blogs seemed to be nothing but self-serving promotional tools, uncritically reveling in the often desperate muck of the "poetry business"—what many of us call "po-biz." To be sure, promotional blogs, like any kind of book marketing strategy, can be useful. Too often, I've fallen into the trap of thinking that my work ends with publication, when actually this is when my work promoting a book begins. Still, I'd question the honesty of anyone who claims po-biz is as satisfying as the reading or making of poems themselves. "Poems endure," as I tell my students, "and po-biz does not."

Back when I first discovered blogging, I was struck by how the rich, journaling nature of the medium went untapped in the many meta-critical takes on po-biz that I read in the blogosphere. As much as I was drawn to the notebook-like nature of Silliman's blog, for instance, I abhorred the sycophantic stream of responses in his comment fields. His blog could generate upwards of 100 comments to an individual posting, most of which nodded in dutiful agreement with whatever Silliman might have been arguing in that day's blog posting. I was disturbed that the diaristic qualities of his blog could seamlessly transform into a venue for poetry's celebrity culture, reaffirming the po-biz authority of Silliman, the poet and poetry critic—even if he was simply posting formulaic reviews of Hollywood blockbusters and reality TV shows—rather than serving as a space for the creation of new writing. (Silliman, too, grew tired of the chatter and bickering in his comment fields, and he eventually closed them down.)

Still, it seemed blogs could do more for my writing process, serving as a diary or notebook but on a public scale. Even with the limitations of blogging evident in sites such as Silliman's, among others, I felt that Shimmy needed an extended, regularly updated blog, and that her blog should be a performance venue as well as a journal, a place where new work could be invented and tinkered with before reshaping it outside the blog for submission to literary journals. This would be a site to channel Shimmy's rage, and to find new spaces for writerly experimentation while still chronicling my life—or, rather, chronicling my life in my disguise as Shimmy.

Chronicling his life . . . disguised as his cat? Oh, please, is he one of *those* writers, so obsessed with his cat that he can't help but anthropomorphize his beloved pet? To some extent, maybe. But I'd suggest that the more pressing issue isn't my obsession with my cat but instead my desire to document my private life in a public notebook that also functioned as a performative space to draft and revise new work. Shimmy's blog, for instance, finally gave me a chance to use the photographs of cattle I had taken in 2004 at the property next door to the Taos, New Mexico, home of Donald Rumsfeld, former U.S. Secretary of Defense and prime architect of the disastrous Iraq War. These photos needed an artistic venue, something beyond the standard online photo album. After watching Alfonso Cuarón's 2001 film *Y Tu Mama Tambien* ("And Your Mama, Too"), I created a five-part serial narrative for the blog, absurdly titled "Y Tu Rumsfeld Tambien." The deliberately ridiculous title was reason enough for me to post the photos, whether or not I wrote text to accompany them. As I "translated" Shimmy's feelings about Rumsfeld (yes, I talked this way, staying in character as the blog's performative translator rather than as mere diarist), it was clear that something more intriguing was at work. A serial narrative was developing.

"Faces and horns, anonymous bodies," Shimmy wrote, "the cattle who live next door to Rumsfeld's home in Taos burst into our apartment. Flies buzzed their rumps." The cattle no longer were anonymous animals living next door to the warmongering Secretary of Defense. Instead, they were panicked creatures trying to escape the nefarious clutches of their terrifying next-door neighbor, as much of the world seemed to be doing when I composed "Y Tu Rumsfeld Tambien" in 2006: "They were running from the Secretary of Defense, fleeing another of his blood ritual masses at the manse in Taos (a Chevy Chevelle sits on blocks in the tall grass next door) where he camped as a Boy Scout in 1948," Shimmy wrote. These facts—the Chevy Chevelle I witnessed in Taos, and my later research on the young Donald Rumsfeld's Boy Scout experiences—eventually found their way into a poem I was writing at the time, "They Sound Bells for Us," a meditation on the limits of family, tribe, and nation that appeared the following year in *The Lama's English Lessons*. I reshaped the final version of "They Sound Bells for Us" from its initial blog draft, its shadow-life as "Y Tu Rumsfeld Tambien"—a draft inhabited by the likes of Rumsfeld, as a blood-dimmed warlock figure straight out of the Satanic mass in Nathaniel Hawthorne's "Young Goodman Brown," and the cattle next door whom Shimmy believed the former Defense Secretary wanted to sacrifice.

As often was the case with Shimmy's blog, where villains tried to charm their way into her prose, Rumsfeld attempted to enchant her:

'Shimmy, come sit on my lap.' It was Rumsfeld, old and plump, tapping his fingers on the arm of the sofa, mimicking the doomed pitter-patter of mice. 'Don't be afraid of me. Look at all these cattle! I'm friends with the animals.'

Shimmy eventually spoke back to Rumsfeld in language appropriated from the texts of Guy Debord, the founder of the postwar French arts movement known as the Situationist International, and Raoul Vaneigem, one of Situationism's major figures. (In the blog, Shimmy secretly had a crush on Debord, whose giant shoes and Gauloise cigarettes made her tail shiver.) Shimmy still couldn't get the Defense Secretary to leave the apartment. Rumsfeld clattered like a poltergeist everywhere in her imagination, herding the cattle with the help of the terrorizing Zuni doll from the 1975 film *Trilogy of Terror*—a sentient doll who stalked Karen Black's character in the film and who was, in Shimmy's mind, the Secretary of Defense's warlock familiar. In Shimmy's world, all Rumsfeld could do was speak in the tortured rhetoric to which the rest of us had grown accustomed during his televised press conferences. "I'm not into this detail stuff—I'm more concepty," he said to her, the same words he delivered in 2002 to the press corps as they questioned the wisdom of the Iraq war.

Although "Y Tu Rumsfeld Tambien" was a serial narrative, I also used Shimmy's blog postings to experiment with nonlinear composition and storytelling, and to hone the appropriation and remixing techniques that still are a deeply felt influence on my writing. A few poems from *Historic Diary* (BlazeVOX [books]), my 2011 documentary poetry collection on the John F. Kennedy assassination, emerged from experiments with disjunction and appropriation that were the foundation of Shimmy's blog. One poem in particular from *Historic Diary*, "*The Manchurian Candidate* (1962)," came directly from my work on Shimmy's blog. I had been experimenting with a posting comprised entirely of questions asked in the original 1962 version of the film *The Manchurian Candidate*, a Cold War thriller whose plot line, the assassination of an American politician by Soviet double agents planted in high positions in the U.S. government, led many to believe it might have served as an inspiration for JFK's alleged assassin, Lee Harvey Oswald. I began the poem by jotting questions asked in the film into Shimmy's blog; as I did so, the questions themselves— lifted from the film and then adapted and remixed in the blog—started to suggest a pattern of narrative disjunction that told a paranoid story of Shimmy's travails with Dr. Kissinger in the notorious Den of Spies:

What's the matter with her? Hey, Shimmy, what about my robe? What's your personal advice? May I take this thing off now, Shimmy?

How many Communists did you say? Can you see the red queen?

You will be taken for a checkup—is that clear? What's your last name? What's your last name? The letter? Have you got the letter?

What sort of greeting is that at 3:30 in the morning? Are you sure they're coming to the party, Shimmy? Are you absolutely sure?

What are you supposed to be, one of those Dutch skaters? Why don't we just sneak away for a few minutes and sit down somewhere quietly and stare out the window?

Shimmy, why don't you pass the time by playing a little solitaire?

Aren't you going to pop champagne, or dance in the streets, or at least slide your food dish around the kitchen floor? Fifty- two red queens and me are telling you—you know what we're telling you?

Seeing these appropriated questions from the film recast in a public, journal-like space of my own—in the blog—helped me shape the material into the poem that later appeared in *Historic Diary*. After I wrote this blog posting, the repetitious nature of the questions suggested to me that I should compose the poem as a pantoum, an obsessively repetitive poetic form that originated in the fifteenth century. The second and fourth lines of each pantoum stanza are repeated as the first and third lines of each subsequent stanza; and the first and third lines of its opening stanza are incorporated as the fourth and second lines, respectively, of its final stanza. As I drafted and revised this nascent pantoum in my word-processing program, the blog posting eventually inspired me to create the poem's final three stanzas, dramatizing the psychological conflict between the film's main character, Raymond Shaw, and his mother (one of the Soviet spies), while also emphasizing the guilt he felt for killing his fellow Korean War soldiers, Ed Mavole and Bobby Lembeck:

Can you see the red queen?
Where are you, Raymond?
Raymond, do you remember murdering Mavole and Lembeck?
Fifty-two red queens and me are telling you—do you know what
    we're telling you?

Where are you, Raymond?
They can make me do anything, Ben, can't they?
Fifty-two red queens and me are telling you—do you know what
    we're telling you?
Ben, you don't blame me for hating my mother, do you?

*"The Queen of Diamonds"? What did she mean, "The Queen of
    Diamonds"?*

May I have the bayonet, please?

Have you ever killed anyone?

Do you know what we're telling you?

The creepy, predatory pitch of Raymond's mother's voice in the
blog posting ("Can you see the red queen? . . . You will be taken for a
checkup—is that clear?") eventually became a model for the poem's
tone. The poem initially was conceived and rehearsed in my "note-
book"—Shimmy's blog—and without such rehearsals, much of the
formal and tonal nuances of the poem might have been lost.

Blogging provides an audience for an artist's untamed journal-
drafts. But given the medium of blogging, its existence within an
extensively searchable range of online content—and the unlimited
potential size of a blog's online audience—a blog also offers the writer
a performative space that combines the childlike (or in Shimmy's
case, the child-arsonist-like) wild-zone of invention with the imme-
diate responsiveness of an audience. Shimmy's blog stretched me
beyond the limits of journaling or letter-writing, because a blog, after
all, can be simultaneously a diary and a piece of performance art.

Shimmy also reviewed movies, an unusual practice for a pri-
vate journal but appropriate for a blog like hers that was part-diary
and part-performance. Her film reviews functioned both as con-
ceptual art pieces and journaling exercises: her reviews consisted
of stream-of-consciousness descriptions of how she, as a house cat,
spent her time alone in the apartment while Shelly and I actually were
at the movie theater. Shimmy's reviews were an extension of my own
fixation with popular culture in my poems—as in *Historic Diary*, where
Soviet and U.S. popular culture embed themselves whenever possi-
ble in Oswald's myths and texts. The blog also reflected the pop-cul-
ture influence of my editorial work as one of the founders and editors
of *Court Green*, a poetry journal that has devoted special sections in

past issues to film poems and political poems, and that every issue publishes a number of poems influenced by popular culture and new media.

Shimmy's child-arsonist blog persona was an invigorating extension of the creative process wild-zone that journaling and letter-writing gives us permission to indulge. The blogosphere was for me a space where the rough drafts of my everyday lived experience and of my writing projects could live on top of each other like palimpsests. It was a space where the writing of a film review, and by extension the writing of poem drafts and all other modes of journaling and performing, could occur simultaneously with the quotidian happenings of my life.

Blogs lost some of their luster with the rise of social media in the late 2000s and early 2010s. Still, blogs persist, and now, roughly a decade after what many consider the golden age of blogging, we are fortunate that with so much diaristic writing being done on blogging and social media platforms, many of the serious writers who continue to work in this medium are truly dedicated to the unusual public-private amalgam of blogging. My favorite contemporary blogs, from veteran writers and editors of poetry and prose, include Joseph Harrington's *The Poem of Our Climate*[1], a continuation of his earlier blog, *Writing Out of Time*[2], both devoted to politically urgent documentation of the ravages of climate change; and Susan M. Schultz's blog[3], a space for her ongoing Buddhist-inspired political writing. Because both Harrington and Schultz are established writers of poetry, prose, and hybrid literature, their blogs feature sophisticated, first-rate, diaristic writing, framed by the intimate spontaneity of a professional writer's notebook.

---

1. www.thepoemofourclimate.weebly.com
2. www.writingoutoftime.weebly.com
3. www.tinfisheditor.blogspot.com

Blogging is by no means a substitute for editorially vetted online or print publication. Many journals, including those I've edited, will not consider work that has been previously published anywhere, including work that already has appeared on a blog. Like most editors, I want to publish work that has not been seen before. Still, blogs can be valuable as public versions of private journals. Blogs combine the potential for both private, undomesticated journaling and public performance. Why else would a writer choose to distribute their private notebooks through a forum that, in its nature as an online publishing platform, includes an audience enormously larger than that of the highest-circulation print literary journals?

In 2010, at the age of sixteen (eighty-one, in human years), Shimmy died of complications from heart disease, kidney disease, hyperthyroidism, and diabetes. Her death coincided with the end of my marriage to Shelly, and the grief from both these losses consumed me. A number of my writer friends good-naturedly suggested that I continue the blog, that Shimmy's persona could still speak to us from the afterlife. But I was too shaken by her death to carry on with it. To some extent, I am indeed one of *those* writers, so attached to my cat that I was compelled to channel her voice. I miss Shimmy. Of my many beautiful memories of her, I'll always be grateful that she curled up on the couch with me every night in December 2008 and binge-watched the first four seasons of *Battlestar Galactica* after Shelly moved out—tender animal moments we shared together in front of the television.

Her final blog posting was, appropriately, part of an extended serial narrative: she pretended to believe that Fox News personality Glenn Beck had been caught perpetuating animal abuse on pit bulls. To anyone remotely following the news at the time, the narrative details of Shimmy's serialized account were a satirical adaptation of professional football star Michael Vick's actual arrest in 2007 for abusing pit bulls as part of a dogfighting ring he helped finance.

(In 2008, Vick pleaded guilty to dogfighting and was sentenced to twenty-three months in federal prison.) Like so many of her postings over the five years she blogged, it was a piece of hybrid flash writing that collaged multiple outside sources into social satire. For this post, Shimmy remixed found material from William Penn's 1670 trial for "preaching in public" with Beck's 2010 keynote address at a conservative political gathering, the "Restore Honor to America Rally" (which, for Beck, was his own form of public preaching). Shimmy was prompted to satirize Beck's "preaching" when she read a news account of the rally in which Beck, a racially insensitive icon of the right wing, compared himself to Martin Luther King, Jr. As far as Shimmy was concerned, Beck was fair game for the kind of narratives we would later call "fake news."

Ever the vandal, Shimmy; always journaling like a child-arsonist, and forever my inspiration for the raw, uncensored, generative potential of performative journaling. Her accusatory posts about Beck often were met with dismay in her comment fields by tin-eared, ironically challenged right-wing bloggers who insisted she provide evidence of Beck's alleged misdeeds. As far as Shimmy was concerned, she was just answering Beck's "fake news" with satirical, fake narratives of her own—tall tales so unbelievable that anyone with a shred of critical thinking skills, let alone a minimal knowledge of unfolding current events at the time, would know were parody. And when the right-wing bloggers would protest too much, demanding empirical evidence from Shimmy that, frankly, they didn't expect from Beck himself, she reminded them in her own comment-field responses that she was only, after all, a simple house cat. Cut her some slack. She could only blog so much before needing a break to recline in a sunbeam.

CHAPTER FOUR

Channeling Other People: The Poet as Medium

Time is the gift of an artists' retreat, and I had plenty of it. I was roughly halfway through a September two-week writing residency at Ragdale, and my only obligation was to meet every evening with the other residents in the main house for a shared dinner. Otherwise, I was on my own to make as much or as little of the gigantic expanse of writing time that awaited me each day. I'm good at budgeting my schedule—writerly stubbornness again, I'm too obstinate to waste available writing time—but in the weeks leading up to the residency, I worried that I might have so much time in front of me that I'd freeze and write nothing at all. I convinced myself that the best approach to the retreat was to give myself permission to write just one good poem while I was there. If I could write one poem that felt finished, I'd consider my time at Ragdale a success.

But here I was, a week into the residency, and I'd already drafted ten pages of *Historic Diary*, a collection of documentary poems that would be published several years later by BlazeVOX. I began the project a year before I arrived at Ragdale. I originally conceived it as a series of four or five poems based on the diary that alleged John F. Kennedy assassin Lee Harvey Oswald kept when he lived in the Soviet Union from 1959 to 1962, a journal he titled "Historic Diary." After just a week at Ragdale, I had written so much that the project was now taking shape as a full-length collection of poems, with most of them spoken in the voices of personas who were important historical figures in the assassination and its aftermath.

The word "persona" derives from the Latin for "mask," and in these persona poems, I wore the masks of a range of major figures from the assassination as a way of exploring the *Rashomon*-like collision of contradictory frames of reference that constitutes our cultural history of JFK's murder. After a week of sustained, uninterrupted writing time at Ragdale, I realized that the persona poem was going to be foundational to the project as a whole, just as it would be, a decade later, for my next documentary poetics collection *Proof Something Happened*. Working that week from materials in Oswald's "Historic Diary," and from government documents in the public domain, I'd just finished a persona poem that re-staged the moment when Oswald and his future wife, Marina, first laid eyes on each other, in 1961 at a dance hall in Minsk. Titled "We Like Each Other Right Away," the poem was written from Oswald's perspective, and was an effort to capture the instant infatuation the two felt the night they met. In order to realistically portray this moment at the Minsk dance hall, I drew on memories of my first date with Shelly in 1985, at a dive bar in Ohio, summoning recollections of the love-at-first-sight hormonal rush I felt that night. I recast the memories of my revved-up emotions from that first date with Shelly to imagine two people on opposite sides of the Cold War lovestruck on *their* first meeting: a defector from the United States falling head-over-heels for a pharmacy technician whose uncle worked for Soviet intelligence.

Not all of my efforts to channel the Oswalds into poetry drew from such romantic personal memories. A few days earlier, I finished a double villanelle, "Marina and Lee," that dramatized the couple's constant arguments in their apartment on Kalinina Street in Minsk. In order to make their combative voices more authentic, I drew from my (sadly) ample experience of marital bickering. Shelly and I weren't getting along well at the time of the residency, and we would split up three years later. I had lots of difficult recent memories to draw on as I dramatized what it felt like to be the Oswalds as they argued with each other in "Marina and Lee." Just as I did with "We Like Each Other Right Away," I used my personal experience, informed by the historical record of the Oswalds' life together, to create a realistic emotional landscape for the poem.

The Ragdale residency had been a prolific one so far, but on this particular day, I found myself stalling. For some reason, I couldn't write. I reread the *Chicago Tribune* at breakfast, wasted time responding to emails that were anything but urgent, doodled in my sketchpad, tried to read a chapter of John Steinbeck's *East of Eden* that was on the shelf of the room where I was staying at Ragdale, and as a last resort to revive my flagging creative energy, I took a long walk on the prairie, a gorgeous, sunny expanse of tallgrass behind the house where I was staying.

It was nearly time for lunch when I returned from the prairie. I wanted to do anything but write—an awful feeling, since I'd spent the previous evening gathering research materials for a poem about Oswald's relationship with his father that I'd planned to start that day.

After more procrastination, and a granola bar and coffee for lunch, I started drafting what eventually became the poem "Oswald, to His Father." The world outside my second-story room in Ragdale's main house dropped away as I immersed myself deeper in drafts and revisions of the poem. The angle of light streaming into my room was changing—my only sense that time was passing—and the early-autumn afternoon sunlight had now given way to an overcast chill. As I worked on the poem, the gray light became more dense, purplish, hinting that dusk was only a couple hours away.

It seems clear to me now, years later, that I'd been stalling that morning because I was scared to write the poem. It's not that I was afraid I couldn't write it well. I didn't feel anxiety about the writing itself. Instead, as I would realize later, my fear was caused by something more primal. I knew I'd have to draw on my own relationship with my father in order to render Oswald's relationship with his. I didn't want to rattle myself by doing the psychological excavation of family memories required to write a poem in which the speaker unearths anxieties and resentments about his father. By avoiding my father that morning at Ragdale, I also was avoiding the poem.

Oswald's relationship with his own father was essentially a communion with a ghost. Oswald's father died when his mother was seven months pregnant with him. As a result, his father was at best a spectral presence in Oswald's life. In a biographical note Oswald penned to "The Kollective," his unpublished 1962 manuscript of life in the Soviet Union, he wrote: "Lee Harvey Oswald was born in Oct. 1939 in New Orleans, La., the son of an insurance salesman whose early death left a far mean streak of independence brought on by neglect." His biographical statement for "The Kollective" was a haunting inspiration for the poem I wanted to write about his relationship with his father, and it guided me through every draft. I trusted that as long as I allowed the writing to be influenced by Oswald's "far mean streak of independence brought on by neglect," the poem would find the shape and voice it required.

But I didn't quite realize how emotionally intense, and artistically vital, it would be to channel *my* father for the poem. I needed to draw on my own "far mean streak of independence brought on by neglect" in order to allow the poem to sound authentically like it was spoken by a man talking to a mute father about paternal detachment.

After trying several different formal strategies for the poem, I eventually decided to compose it as a letter from Oswald to his father. I consider letters and emails to be the most intimate and uninhibited forms of writing we can do. They are unmediated forms of connection with one's audience—simply one person talking directly to another without worrying about whether or not the words are coming out with polish or élan. I was confident that the uninhibited nature of letter-writing would provide a stage for portraying how Oswald's childhood trauma shaped the man he became. I imagined it as a letter-poem whose significant physical distance (the son talking back to the father who died before he was born) and political distance (the Cold-War-defector-son writing to the dead father he believed had abandoned him) would enact the emotional and physical loss that shaped Oswald's personality from childhood.

As I continued to revise "Oswald, to His Father," the light from outside waning, it was becoming clear that I also needed to confront the unsettling domestic violence inherent in Oswald's "far mean streak"—the historically documented fact that he frequently beat Marina. I was fortunate to grow up in a household in which no family members physically attacked each other. Within my extended family, it's a different story altogether. I have too many childhood memories of hotheaded uncles and cousins raising a hand to their spouses at family gatherings. I've seen the fear on their spouses' faces—and the self-loathing on these uncles' and cousins' faces in the aftermath, as they realized they'd just exposed their private family violence to the outside world. In order to imagine the atmosphere of domestic violence in the Oswalds' home, I turned to the cruelties of those uncles and cousins as a model.

Oswald's loss, a father whom he literally never saw in the flesh, was more profound than my own, of course; my father's absence was emotional, not physical. My father was a benign presence in our home, but his emotions were barricaded and inaccessible to me. Every day, he came home exhausted from the steel factory where he worked. I did everything I could as a child to get his attention, at times climbing on his lap and slapping the newspaper he was reading so that he would put down the paper and show me his face. But factory life, as I would find out myself in a short stint in the mid-1980s working second shift at a plastics plant, is physically draining and can be emotionally debilitating. Whether or not he was consciously aware that he wasn't giving me the emotional attention I needed, he was too tired every night to do anything about it.

Born in 1921, he was a product of Depression-era gender norms, and he understood fatherhood primarily in terms of breadwinning. Fathers hardened their sons for a world that wore down its men with long hours at factories and mills, with the hope that the sons would work at a union shop (he did not) or for an employer who generously offered weekend and holiday shifts that paid time-and-a-half (he took as much time-and-a-half as he could). If I complained, wanting more from him, and more from a world in which we lived paycheck-to-paycheck, his response was the fatalistic cliché, "Life isn't a bowl of cherries," a phrase that baffled me because I detested cherries. If a bowl of cherries is our standard against which we judge our aspirations, then it was nothing more than a misery index for an inevitably depressing future. I had no desire for life to be a bowl of cherries (please, make it sweet strawberries or juicy diced cantaloupe). I didn't understand that he was trying to be the best father he could, given his conception of how fathers should raise sons. He felt duty-bound to prepare me not to want a life of cherries, strawberries, cantaloupe, or whatever else might seem luxurious and therefore unattainable.

"Oswald, to His Father" began to take shape as a poem once I recognized that Oswald and I both were emotionally stunted by fathers who were absent because of circumstances no one in the family, especially the fathers themselves, could control. As a result, we spent much of our lives trying to find fathers who weren't really there. Oswald's father's early death, along with my father's social conditioning that a son becomes a man by neglecting his emotional development, were both, as I write in the poem, "safe, virtuous desertion[s]."

I usually require weeks, or even months, before I can shepherd a poem from an early-draft state into something closer to a final version. But as I sensed the afternoon giving way to early evening, and with dinner just a couple hours away, I felt that the poem was nearly finished. I couldn't think of much more that it needed (as it turns out, I was correct, and the version I completed that afternoon at Ragdale was more or less the one that would appear in the book). I decided to take a rest, maybe even a nap, with the confidence that I'd eventually be hungry enough for my body to rouse itself when it was time for dinner.

I awoke in the dark, disoriented. Looked at the clock. It was nine in the evening. I'd slept through dinner. I wasn't remotely hungry, though, and was suffering from stomach cramps and a terrible headache, as if I'd been drinking all afternoon instead of writing a poem. Maybe I was coming down with a cold or flu. I forced myself downstairs to the Ragdale kitchen and made myself a couple slices of toast. I managed a few bites. Couldn't believe how dry my mouth was. I drank nearly a full pitcher of water before I felt a semblance of physical and mental energy return.

Back in my room, I called Shelly and talked about my strange afternoon—my excitement at finishing the poem, and, later, my confusion at how sick I felt afterward.

"You were channeling your own father as you channeled Oswald's," she said. "Who wouldn't be exhausted after something like that?"

She was right. I hadn't approached Oswald's relationship with his father with the sober distance of, for example, a work of historical scholarship. Instead, I had made myself vulnerable enough—as a psychic medium might—for both Oswald's and my own identities to be superimposed on one another in a poem. I'd channeled Oswald and his physically absent father through my difficult memories of my own emotionally absent father. As Shelly said, who wouldn't be exhausted after something like that?

No wonder I slept through dinner that day at Ragdale and felt hungover from writing a poem.

I've mentioned before that my father was raised in a family of musicians but couldn't quite understand why his son would aspire to make a life as a musician and a writer. Even though he supported my artistic talent in music, he didn't expect me to choose the life of an artist, which seemed to him a dangerous decision to make in a country such as ours that, it sometimes seems, distrusts the arts. What's more, his son, the man spending two weeks at Ragdale working on persona poems for a book based on the myths and texts of the JFK assassination, also had devoted most of his adult working life to teaching the art of writing. Not only was I making dangerous life choices, I was mentoring my writing students as they did the same.

Still, I loved my father and he loved me. Even as I write this now, more than a decade after his death (so long ago that I can barely remember what his voice sounded like), I find myself missing him at some point in every day. He was the most patient person I've ever met, and one of the most disciplined—two traits that, along with his legendary stubbornness that I've discussed earlier, have served me well as a writer.

"Oswald, to His Father" depends on exactly this kind of complicated family dynamic. Both Oswald's father and my own couldn't be blamed for their absences, for the "safe, virtuous desertion[s]" that provide the poem with much of its emotional tension. Neither father truly deserted his son. But to Oswald and me, young boys not fully understanding the worlds we were born into, our fathers' respective absences felt like desertions—a metaphor I was slowly beginning to see as a foundation for the poem. Here's the poem as it appears in *Historic Diary*:

Oswald, to His Father

I hit Marina. Can't help it, the way
she holds the baby. When the pacifier falls

on the floor, she cleans it with her mouth—
she can't see the drift of microbes.

The floors are dirty and must be washed
every day. They tell me you sold
insurance, you know what I mean—
if you keep things clean, you don't need

to gamble with a premium, a briefcase,
some rickety box of soul we call
property. I could not tell Mother
about my plans because she could hardly

be expected to understand. Say something,
Father, to give me back the moonlight
from the rafters. When they told me about
you, I was a burst tub gashed with an axe,

sweet beer sloshing. They said you died
two months before I was born.
A safe, virtuous desertion.
I'd spell out what I mean for you

if I could. Let me put it this way.
I'm supposed to believe this world
was made by a father who turned
one son against the other

over slaughtered sheep and a bundle
of hay? No, we've made it here: at night
we watch the Svisloch River from the balcony,
grazing the green banks of Kalinina Street.

It's February in Minsk but I'm so sweaty
I'd like to grab a rocking chair

for a breeze. I feel like an old man.
Marina's eye is black. Junie's crying.

It might seem unusual that I'm using the dramatic word "chan-
neling" to describe my effort to craft authentic personas for history-
based poems. The word "channeling" is used primarily to describe
what psychics or mediums purport to do. They claim to serve as
intermediaries between the material world and the spiritual world,
summoning the consciousness of someone who has passed away
and then functioning as a vessel through which the deceased con-
sciousness can speak. Psychics and mediums tend to report a terrific
exhaustion caused by their otherworldly communion with the dead,
and this bone-weary fatigue often can be seen as proof of the verac-
ity of their work. I make no claim to being a psychic poet, nor is this
chapter an effort to explore whether or not extrasensory perception
actually exists. But if psychics are legit, then it follows that serving
as an intermediate host for a deceased consciousness—rather than,
for instance, just fabricating fraudulent details of a dead loved one's
afterlife journey—would be an absolutely grueling process. Essen-
tially, you're allowing your consciousness to be temporarily colonized
by a host parasite, and, to recall what Shelly said to me on the phone
that night at Ragdale, how could this be anything but exhausting? It
just hadn't occurred to me that writing a poem might produce the
same kind of knocked-out fatigue that mediums report after a ses-
sion channeling the dead.

The persona poet has to become—only up to a certain point—the
persona they are speaking through. To create the conditions for a
three-dimensional human being to emerge from the language and
imagery of a persona poem, I need to be unguarded enough to allow
myself to be taken over (almost) by the persona at the core of the
poem. I don't want the other consciousness to inhabit me full-time,
just as a medium summoning the spirit world eventually wants to

return at some point to their ordinary, everyday identity, too. When I wrote "Oswald, to His Father," I managed to stop just short of being possessed by my persona. Had I lost myself completely in Oswald's voice, or in turn, had I immersed myself too deeply in memories of my fraught relationship with my father, I wouldn't have been able to finish the poem at all. As exotic as the channeling metaphor might seem, no good can come from—and I doubt any good writing can come from—allowing yourself to dissolve completely into someone else. If I make myself too vulnerable while channeling the voices of others, I risk disappearing; yet, if I clamp down too hard on my own voice in an effort to avoid being possessed, I'll go too far in the other direction and find myself unable to create a believable persona who exists independent of my own experience. I'd been vulnerable enough to allow Oswald's persona to cross a bridge into my consciousness when I composed the poem, but I was also mindful that, as the writer, I was in control of this bridge between self and other. The writer decides when to send the persona back across the bridge, and, if necessary, to dismantle the bridge once the persona has departed.

.

I often draw on family experiences when creating personas. For most of us, our earliest intimate relationships are with family members, and our parent-figures become archetypes for how we experience friendships and relationships in adulthood. But I don't mean to suggest that channeling a persona for a piece of writing is as self-enclosed and private as families themselves tend to be. Persona poetry also requires an historical accuracy, and to create an authentic persona I must be aware that the private psychological tensions of a life always occur within an historical context. Our complex internal lives cannot be separated from the historical moment in which we are living.

Claudia Rankine and Beth Loffreda discuss this convergence of the private and the historical in their 2017 essay "The Racial Imaginary." "While it might be mystifying how creative impulses and deci-sions emerge from somewhere within," they write, "that doesn't mean we must make a fetish of that mysteriousness. For that unknow-able portion of the human mind is also a domain of culture—a place crossed up by culture and history, where the conditions into which we are born have had their effect." In this sense, "history" is more than a series of events that make up a chronological period of time. History is also a matter of how we negotiate our chronological era within the context of "the conditions into which we are born"—the racial, sexual, gender, class, and ability identities that help shape who we are. Even though this chapter is framed by the metaphor of the persona poet as a psychic medium, I don't believe it requires an act of the supernatural to exert the imaginative effort required to empa-thize with another human being deeply enough to represent them aesthetically as a persona. It is, instead, like all the work of the imag-ination, an historical act. Writing a persona poem requires sensitivity and dexterity with matters of both craft and historical accuracy. That is, with both the imagination and what Rankine and Loffreda call the "domain of culture—a place crossed up by culture and history." When I write from the perspective of a persona, no matter how immersed I am in the seemingly private space of my imagination, I am always an historical being. As my earliest mentors taught me, the personal is political—to which I would add, the personal is also historical.

Still, it's not enough for me to be mindful that my seemingly pri-vate imagination is conditioned by my historical moment. Creating an authentic persona also requires empathy in order to channel other people without othering them. In his 1821 essay "A Defense of Poetry," Percy Bysshe Shelley argues that poetry strengthens our capacity to empathize with others "in the same manner as exercise strengthens a limb." The kind of empathy required for writing a persona poem is more than simply imagining oneself in the situations that others have found themselves in. Instead, it is an effort to go out of oneself, temporarily, and imagine the three-dimensional psychological and emotional world of someone else. This complicated relationship between ourselves and our personas is taken up by Stacey Lynn Brown and Oliver de la Paz in the introduction to their 2012 volume, *A Face to Meet the Faces: An Anthology of Contemporary Persona Poetry*. The persona poem is "at its heart, an act of empathy," they write, "of walking that mile in someone else's shoes to determine not only what the view is like from there, but what those shoes, and that body, *feel* like." When I write in the mask of a persona, I am not so much writing *about* that persona as I am writing *with* that persona. I am writing about "what the view is like from there," but, more important, I'm also writing with the intimate sensation of "what those shoes, and that body, *feel* like." The poet is inevitably changed by the persona-writing process, Brown and de la Paz argue: "Truly inhabiting the consciousness of someone else heightens our own and makes us more aware of our own predispositions, prejudices, and predilections." We are necessarily changed by the process of writing while wearing the mask of another person. Blurring the boundary between myself and my personas implicates me in their stories, too; and most of all, it prevents me from treating my personas as if they were specimens in a natural history exhibit.

In a culture that increasingly embraces the echo chambers of social media, where we can mute or unfollow anyone whose opinions differ from our own, the empathy required for writing the persona poem looks more radical to me each day. "Oswald, to His Father," for instance, required that I find nonjudgmental common ground with an alleged assassin, which, in turn, required me to face the uncomfortable reality of the mutual "far mean streak[s] of independence and neglect" that shaped our boyhoods. I found the process unsettling, in the least, but writing the poem helped me understand how my childhood relationship with my father contributed to the adult I've become. Superimposing Oswald's feelings of "independence and neglect" with my own helped me come to terms with the simple truth that fathers raise us the best they can, conditioned for better or worse by the historical periods in which they're raised; and seeing my own father in this context affirmed that our relationship was one of mutual love. Without this kind of empathy, I couldn't have written any of the persona poems in *Historic Diary* and *Proof Something Happened*. On the surface, adopting the persona mask could seem like a gesture of concealment, offering the writer a chance to hide in the consciousness of someone else. I'd suggest the opposite is true. We make some of our most important discoveries about ourselves and our historical moment when we go out of ourselves to summon the voices of others for our poems.

CHAPTER FIVE

Writing Poems with (Emotional) History in Them

I was visiting Ruth Paine in 2006 at the retirement community where she lives on the West Coast, interviewing her over lunch as part of my research for *Historic Diary*. Paine, a devout and socially conscious Quaker, was unwittingly swept up in the events surrounding John F. Kennedy's assassination on November 22, 1963, and, as a result, the details of her ordinary, everyday life are now indelible parts of the official historical record. With Paine's permission, I'd brought to the interview my cousin Michael Trigilio, my closest family member, a multimedia artist who is as deeply interested in the history of the assassination as I am. The three of us sat in Paine's modest living room eating salads purchased earlier at the retirement center's cafeteria and talking about Paine's experiences with Marina Oswald and her husband Lee Harvey Oswald.

Paine met the Oswalds in the spring of 1963, and she and Marina quickly developed a friendship. Later that year, while separated from Lee, Marina accepted an invitation from Paine to stay temporarily at her home in Irving, Texas, while the Oswalds tried to repair their marriage. Marina brought along her one-year-old daughter, June, and was pregnant with her second child, Rachel (who would be born a month before the assassination, while Marina was still living in the Paine household).

Like the Oswalds, Paine and her husband also were separated at the time, though it was a more amicable split than Marina and Lee's. Paine welcomed the company of Marina and her children.

"It was nice to have another young mother with little kids," she said as we discussed the period in fall 1963 leading up to the assassination. "Someone to hang diapers with. Fold them, too."

Marina was living in Paine's home on the day Kennedy was shot, and the two of them watched the initial, chaotic news coverage on television in the living room. And, yes, Marina was hanging diapers—her children's and Ruth's—on the backyard clothesline later that afternoon when Paine came outside to relay an important news update: the Dallas police believed that JFK had been shot by a sniper firing from an upper-story window of the Texas School Book Depository, where Lee worked. It was Ruth who innocently had suggested he apply for the job earlier that fall, after hearing from a neighbor that the Depository was hiring.

The stories Paine told of her day-to-day life in 1963 were situated squarely at the intersection of our official and unofficial histories of the assassination. Paine described giving driving lessons to Lee Harvey Oswald in the weeks prior to the assassination, a detailed narrative I adapted for the poem "He Needed a Learner's Permit." We spent much of our time talking about the effect the assassination had on her family. I asked about how Quaker practice helped her cope with the aftermath, as she and her husband became the objects of intensive media scrutiny. One of the reasons I was interested in interviewing Paine was her serious, lifelong spiritual commitment. Most of the major figures in the history of the assassination seemed avowedly secular to me or, at the least, appeared to be non-practicing members of their respective religions. Paine was the exception. I was curious to know how her religious practice shaped her response to the assassination and the unwelcome historical limelight.

"Spiritual life got me through the event, in a sense," she said, "but not just the spiritual life. I think I was very fortunate that I had certain strengths that I didn't think I had but were there. One was that I liked the news media. I believe in democracy and what the press does and their role. So, I didn't feel invaded [by the media]."

We continued to talk about how she and her family dealt with the attention brought upon them by the assassination and its aftermath. After a time, the conversation shifted to her Quaker-inspired activism of the 1980s. We talked, too, about the 9/11 attacks and how national tragedies such as this, and the JFK assassination, affected the country's collective psyche. As I spooned a few remaining iceberg lettuce leaves and chickpeas from my plate, I noticed Paine moving and shifting her legs restlessly underneath the dining room table. My questions were relatively benign, I assumed, but watching Paine become jittery, crossing and re-crossing her legs, I couldn't help but think that the interview was causing her considerable distress.

"We don't have to keep the interview going," I said. "I don't want my questions to make you uncomfortable. It's no problem for us to stop."

"One of the things I begin to notice is that I do begin to shake when I have this conversation. I only do it two or three times max in a year because it costs emotionally to do it."

I was passionate about talking to her for the book, but I didn't want the interview to occur at the expense of Paine's health. Back when I was a journalist, I never got comfortable sticking a tape recorder in someone's face and asking them how they felt about a newsworthy trauma they'd just experienced.

"I feel it's appropriate," she added. "You didn't twist my arm. But it's emotionally expensive."

We continued the interview.

I didn't realize until much later that, while Paine and I had shared lunch that day and talked about the effects of the assassination on her—and on the country as a whole—we had unintentionally come up with a shared vocabulary for how poetry can effectively document an historical event.

"You're doing something different," she said as we brought the interview to a close. "You're writing a history that's based in the *emotions*."

.

Writing *Historic Diary* and, later, *Proof Something Happened*, taught me just how personal this seemingly distant thing called "history" can actually be. Writing poems based in history is, as Paine suggested, a process of "writing a history that's based in the emotions." Yet, like many contemporary poets, my earliest, foundational reading was in the autobiographical lyric, a poetic mode that generally de-emphasizes history in order to focus on the inner life of its first-person speaker. At its most basic level, the contemporary lyric unfolds as a short, compact meditation in which the "I" (often a barely veiled persona for the poet) reflects on the complicated relationship between the narrator's psyche and the outside world as the poem builds toward an epiphany in which the noisy inner life of the poet collides with an indifferent natural world. The lyric poem is important to me. It's essentially the default poetic form when I'm not writing persona or documentary-based work. But the privatized space of the lyric "I" doesn't adequately represent for me the more complex process of reading (and writing) the day-to-day experience of one's historical moment. I need to augment the inward-seeking voice of the lyric with poems whose narrative personas are self-aware of the historical moment in which they live.

Back when I first began to read and write poetry as a serious art form, I encountered individual stand-alone persona poems, and I was excited by the ways persona poets collaged the voices of others with their own. But it wasn't until much later, in graduate school, that I discovered entire book-length projects in which the poet's voice, the voices of others, and the emotional urgencies of history could merge into one. I didn't know that full-length books of poetry could include narrative voices in a collage of historical personas in addition to the conventional, singular voice of a private, lyrical subjectivity. This kind of work is known as "documentary poetry" for the aesthetic and journalistic tendencies it shares with documentary film.

I had no idea that entire long-form poetry projects like this could be written until I took a workshop in graduate school with Robin Becker, a poet whose mentorship was invaluable to my development as a reader and writer. One of the books we read for the class was Pamela Alexander's *A Commonwealth of Wings*, a collection of persona poems on the life and work of nineteenth-century naturalist and artist John James Audubon. I wasn't necessarily entranced with Audubon as a historical figure (it was in Alexander's book where I first learned, to my horror, that Audubon shot and killed every bird he brought to life in his paintings). I was moved, instead, by Alexander's deft ability as a poet-historian-biographer. She documents Audubon's life with the kind of narrative coherence we expect from historical texts, while also guided by the psychological realism and emotional vulnerability that is a tendency of contemporary lyric poetry.

Soon after reading and studying Alexander's book, I discovered W.D. Snodgrass's 1977 poetry collection, *The Fuehrer Bunker*, a volume of dramatic monologues that portray life in Hitler's bunker during the last days of the Third Reich. The book, spoken in the personas of the historical figures who hid themselves in the bunker as Allied armies advanced toward Berlin, unfolds in a variety of formal verse and choral modes whose structural tensions add an even more sinister element to the historical drama of the poems.

Of course, I took no pleasure in the historical personas, all devoted

Nazis, who narrate the poems of *The Fuehrer Bunker*. Snodgrass's collection is devastating primarily because it historicizes individual pathology; the poems, as dramatic monologues, provide a stage for their repellant speakers to freely incriminate themselves. Magda Goebbels's justification of the poisoning of the family's children in the poem "This is the needle that we give" still unsettles me decades after my first reading of it. "Open wide, now, little bird," Snodgrass's Magda says to her children as she murders them in the name of Hitler: "I who sang you your first word / Soothe away every sound you've heard / Except your Leader's voice." The poems in *The Fuehrer Bunker* do not try to justify or absolve the actions of their bunkered Nazis, nor do they excuse the menacing, often sadistic epiphanies of their narrators. The book's center of gravity, instead, is history itself. *The Fuehrer Bunker* invites us to explore history as only a poem can—that is, a history told in subjective flash-cut scenes, in colliding, associative voices from multiple personas, in scraps of language and imagery, and in found archival material.

Rather than proffer the tidy historical narratives featured in textbooks, Alexander's and Snodgrass's collections helped teach me the extent to which historical narrative is imposed after the fact. The emotional realism of their historicized lyric speakers reminds us that history unfolds instead in the messy immediate present of nonlinear, sometimes impulsive, human action.

At first glance, history can seem to be nothing but a series of chronological events that were fated to happen. We might think, for example, it was inevitable that the rise of fascism after World War I would lead to World War II, and that the defeat of the Axis powers in World War II was as destined as the subsequent decade of prosperity that many of the victorious countries experienced afterward. As a child, watching the Watergate hearings on television with my mother, and later, seeing President Richard Nixon's resignation speech on TV with my whole family, I assumed that Nixon's downfall was fated from the start. I was too young to know any better. But the events leading to the exposure of Nixon's transgressions and to his eventual resignation were, instead, the product of imperfect, flawed human beings trying our best to govern ourselves—sometimes succeeding, and often making a shamble of things. As I write this, the House of Representatives continues to hold hearings on the January 6, 2021, insurrection at the United States Capitol. Selected hearings have been broadcast by two of the country's twenty-four-hour news networks. No matter how alluring it might be to construct a tidy narrative of closure about January 6—a linear story with an easily identifiable beginning, middle, and end—it'll be inaccurate to describe the eventual historical outcome as inevitable or fated. "The forces operating in history," writes cultural theorist and historian Michel Foucault, "are not controlled by destiny or regulative mechanisms, but respond to haphazard conflicts." Even though we often turn to memoir and fiction for personalized accounts of such "haphazard conflicts," Alexander's and Snodgrass's books suggested that I could experience them in poetry, too.

As a young writer immersed in the first-person narrative lyric mode, it was a revelation for me to encounter *A Commonwealth of Wings* and *The Fuehrer Bunker*. These books of documentary poetry were breakthrough moments in reading that many poets can recognize—instances when you say to yourself, "How come it never occurred to me that I can write a poem about *that?*"

The documentary poet's materials tend to be the overlooked details of everyday lived experience: the mundane archive of our personal lives—diaries and correspondence, especially—that often are de-emphasized when a linear narrative is imposed on the otherwise chaotic happenings that constitute what we call "history." Such is the case, for instance, with my book *Proof Something Happened*, published in 2021 by Marsh Hawk Press, a collection of documentary poems based on the alleged UFO abduction of Betty and Barney Hill in 1961 from New Hampshire's White Mountains. The book's subject matter is the Hills themselves as they navigate their traumatic historical moment, trying to convince a skeptical public that something did indeed happen to them in the White Mountains. The history of the Hills also must be understood in the context of American racism and white supremacy. I could not adequately explore this history in my poems without researching archival materials such as the couple's correspondence and Betty Hill's journals. An interracial couple, the Hills struggled to be taken seriously in a white supremacist culture poised to dismiss outright the fantastical tale of their alleged alien encounter. *Proof Something Happened* is not an effort to solve the mystery of the Hills' alleged abduction. Whether or not the abduction actually occurred is less important to the poems than the Hills' efforts in subsequent years to make sense of their experience within a skeptical, racist culture.

Alexander's and Snodgrass's books were archetypal poetry collections that led me to write documentary poems like those in *Proof Something Happened* and *Historic Diary*. They helped me generate work that could be immersed in the lyric poem's commitment to documenting its speaker's relationship to the external world, while at the same time historicizing this relationship.

.

In his preface to the 1800 edition of *Lyrical Ballads*, William Wordsworth famously described poetry as "the spontaneous overflow of powerful feelings" that "takes its origin from emotion recollected in tranquility." With apologies to Wordsworth, my early reading in documentary poetics revealed how the lyric impulse in poetry does not have to limit itself only to a private "spontaneous overflow of powerful feelings." Documentary poems seemed to emerge from an intensity and pressure even greater than "emotion recollected in tranquility." Alexander and Snodgrass gave me permission to write a lyric poem whose speaking subject—in all of its "spontaneous overflow"—could not be extricated from its historical moment.

The documentary work I've read since Robin's class has shaped my writing in ways that, years later, I'm only beginning to understand. These books include Ed Sanders's *Investigative Poetry*, a veritable how-to guide for the documentary poet, and the following volumes (a subjective list, not meant to be an exhaustive account of the numerous documentary poetics volumes published in the last few decades): Theresa Hak Kyung Cha, *Dictee*; Martha Collins, *Blue Front*; Nicole Cooley, *The Afflicted Girls*; Eve L. Ewing, *1919*; Diane Gilliam Fisher, *Kettle Bottom*; Joseph Harrington, *Things Come On: An Amneoir*; Tyehimba Jess, *Olio*; A. Van Jordan, *M-A-C-N-O-L-I-A*; Dolores Kendrick, *The Women of Plums*; Adrian Matejka, *The Big Smoke*; Maggie Nelson, *Jane: A Murder*; Mark Nowak, *Shut Up Shut Down* and *Coal Mountain Elementary*; Craig Santos Perez's multivolume *unincorporated territory* series; Charles Reznikoff's *Holocaust* and *Testimony*; Muriel Rukeyser, *The Book of the Dead*; and C.D. Wright, *One with Others*. These are books that combine, often in hybrid poetry/prose forms, an individual lyric voice with a commitment to history, which, in turn, suggests a modification—at times, an outright rejection—of the excessively private voice that can dominate the contemporary lyric mode. As these books capture the historically contingent, emotionally rich life lived within a particular era, they re-center the unofficial histories too often suppressed in the name of a culture's governing master narratives.

I read widely in the documentary mode because I'm not satisfied with the binary opposition between poetry and public life that too often seems fundamental to the autobiographical lyric. The documentary poem is an aesthetically generative space—and a thematically unsettling one, given the cruelties of human history—where language can be intensely personal and emotional while also representing the disjunctive experience of the individual self in history.

When I'm working on a documentary poetics project, I try to personalize the experience of history so that it emerges from human feeling and not from musty textbooks. I'm equally as interested in official historical documents as in unofficial ones. At the core, I'm focused on truth-telling, since documentary poetry is, for me, the literary equivalent of a documentary film. In this way, my source material necessarily includes government documents and newspaper and television reports, along with more conventional historical texts. But it's just as important that I turn to more subjective, emotional kinds of truth, like one-on-one interviews, diaries, journals, and correspondence. I'm especially drawn to how the unofficial history of an event can emerge from personal correspondence. When most of us write letters and emails to friends, we're not really worried about what we're going to say. We tend to express ourselves more freely in such instances, since the uninhibited, nonjudgmental space of a letter or email gives us permission to be more open and vulnerable than we might feel in other, more formal kinds of communication. Correspondence is essentially unrestricted first-draft writing, and as a result, letters and emails often reveal more about ourselves and our historical moment than we might think. Truths tend to leak out more in correspondence than in writing that is self-consciously curated, edited, and reshaped. I don't mean to suggest that the so-called "official" histories we find, for example, on the front page of the *New York Times* are unimportant. The official history is vital. But when I'm working on a documentary poetics project, I try to keep in mind that the official history is only one side of a multifaceted story. The official history often represents the status quo version of an historical event, a foundational version of history that the documentary poet needs to know but is by no means the final word on what happened. Documentary poets are aware of the historical narrative accepted as a mainstream, collective truth. But we know, too, that individuals rarely experience history in the way it is described in official accounts. We often create a coherent narrative of our era in subjective artifacts like diaries and corre-spondence, which is why I find it vital to combine both the official and unofficial truths of an historical event when I'm researching and writ-ing in the documentary mode.

In order to thoroughly dramatize this collision of official and unof-ficial histories, I also include as much of my own personal experience as I can in my documentary poems. My hope is to blur the bound-ary between myself and my subject matter so that my documentary poems are also an account of me trying to write ethically about oth-ers—my effort to write about other people without othering them, as I describe this process in the previous chapter. In this way, a documen-tary poetics project can be more than just an investigation of an his-torical event; it also can be an exploration of history itself as a series of messy, sometimes haphazard, shared emotional narratives.

In *Historic Diary*, this strategy of implicating myself in the histor-ical narrative wasn't just a matter of superimposing Oswald's and my own childhood experiences. It also meant that I included first-person poems in which I tried to understand for myself why I was so inter-ested in writing about the JFK assassination in the first place. No sur-prise, the answer was partly rooted in family history. My mother and brother frequently talked about watching Dallas nightclub impresa-rio Jack Ruby shoot Lee Harvey Oswald on live television the Sun-day after Oswald had been arrested. I lamented that I was born three years too late to share this paradigm-shifting experience with them.

Much the same is true with *Proof Something Happened*, which I began shortly after my father died. The poem "Sightings Journal," for instance, pivots back and forth between Betty Hill's journals and my final visit with my father at the nursing home where he would die three weeks later. Inserting myself into the book's narrative helped me see that Betty and Barney Hill's experience in the White Moun-tains was more than a UFO captivity narrative. Most of all, it was a story of love and loss, as seen especially in Betty's journals. Her efforts to track repeated sightings of unidentified aerial phenomena reveal her intense grief for Barney, who died from a stroke eight years after their alleged abduction and a decade before she began keeping a journal. The grief between the lines in Betty's journal was especially sensitive to me at the time, in my earliest stages of mourning my father.

It seemed that Betty was trying to bring Barney to life in the journal, as I was trying to do with my father in the poem. Our experiences in grief-writing collide as the poem comes to a close:

Betty stands at the edge of the railroad tracks, watching the stars.
She logged 2,998 UFO sightings, 204 trips to the tracks in Exeter,
    between 1983 and 1989.
"Actual count," she writes on the journal's first page, "less than
    those actually seen."
I tried not to use the past tense when we spoke. I didn't want him
    to feel like everything was already over.
The crossword lately made him dizzy.
We didn't talk much. I had to leave an hour later to catch a plane
    back to Chicago.
My god, how we wreck ourselves keeping the dead alive.

CHAPTER SIX

Writing What You Don't Know

I'd just sat down for an office-hour appointment in early-fall 1993 with my Northeastern University graduate school mentor, the scholar and poet Guy Rotella. After some small talk, Guy asked me what I'd been reading for my upcoming Ph.D. exams in twentieth-century poetry and poetics. I took out the list of specialized scholarly monographs and poetry collections I had prepared with him the previous semester. I told him that I was reading Carey Nelson's *Repression and Recovery: Modern American Poetry and the Politics of Cultural Memory, 1910–1945*, and that I just returned to David Perkins's *A History of Modern Poetry, Volume II: Modernism and After*. As for poets, I was reading John Ashbery's *Flow Chart* and Lyn Hejinian's *My Life*, and I just finished Robert Creeley's *Collected Poems* in preparation a reading Creeley was giving at Northeastern later that semester.

As an afterthought, I said that I just devoured Charles E. Shepard's *Forgiven: The Rise and Fall of Jim Bakker and the PTL Ministry*, a 1989 exposé on the sex scandals that brought down Jim and Tammy Faye Bakker's *PTL Club* televangelist empire.

"That's right," Guy said, "I forgot you are drawn to arcana."

At the time, I was startled by how deeply Guy's remark revealed my own emerging poetics to myself. It could've seemed like a backhanded dismissal, but I understood his remark as one of the highest compliments I could receive, an acknowledgment of my wide range of reading influence, from the literary (Creeley) to the arcane (Bakker). No other mentor has exerted the kind of impact on my writing that Guy had. He recognized my eclecticism as a reader and writer before I did, saw that my interests often veer so far from the center of official verse culture that they could rightly be categorized as eccentric or arcane. This is what our best mentors do, take it upon themselves to help us discover our aesthetic (in this case, my desire to fuse the center and the margins, the authorized and the arcane) before we even know what it is. I still treasure this moment of visibility as a writer and artist.

Like most writers, I try to read more than I think I need to—then to read even more—and to read not just in literary genres outside of poetry, but also in what otherwise might seem peculiar or even crackpot. I find the most exciting and original source material often resides in liminal texts that thrive outside the so-called literary center—the mysterious, the eccentric, the trashy. *Forgiven: The Rise and Fall of Jim Bakker and the PTL Ministry* was gossipy and scandalous, and this alone was enough for it to serve as an early muse. I had been waiting for something to topple the Bakkers' Ozymandias-like empire ever since I realized in high school that my mother was secretly donating money to the Bakkers' fundraising drive to build a religious-based theme park.

Shephard's detailed history of the PTL Club provided important background material years later for the poem "Bibles for Vietnam," an account of my high school years watching *The PTL Club* with my mother that appeared in my first collection of poems, *The Lama's English Lessons*. I am a high school senior in the poem, watching *The PTL Club* with my mother before school. That day's episode features a Vietnam veteran describing for Bakker his harrowing battlefield religious conversion, a redemption tale that the poem entangles with the narrative of my growing suspicion (later proved to be true) about my mother's secret PTL donations. "She gave to his theme park," my teenage self discovers at the end of the poem, "committed us in monthly payments, / clandestine phone calls from the kitchen // when Tammy Faye sang 'We're Blessed' / at the end of every broadcast."

My attraction to the arcane has deepened over the years into a poetics that closely reflects the historical roots of the word "arcane" itself—specifically, its original association with the mysterious and obscure, derived in part from language once used to describe the esoteric practices of early modern European alchemists. My documentary poetry collection *Historic Diary* incorporates archival materials ranging from government documents to books and essays that reside on the plausible margins of JFK assassination research. For my ongoing multivolume experiment in autobiography, *The Complete* Dark Shadows *(of My Childhood)*—the third volume published in 2019 by BlazeVOX, and the fourth in progress—I am still watching episodes of the 1960s soap opera *Dark Shadows* and incorporating gossipy daytime soap kitsch and vampire lore into long-form, hybrid poetry/prose.

My most recent volume of poetry, *Proof Something Happened*, is inspired by a different kind of arcana: the post-World War II flying saucer phenomenon. As I've mentioned earlier, the book, also a collection of documentary poems, explores the alleged UFO abduction of Betty and Barney Hill in New Hampshire's White Mountains in 1961. The poems take no stand on the possibility of extraterrestrial life and alien abduction. The collection presumes only that the three hours of "missing time" the Hills experienced in the White Mountains truly did happen psychologically, whether caused by an alien abduction or something else on the fringes of the known. As the poems explore the aftermath of that evening in 1961, they emphasize the Hills' struggle to understand their terrifying dreams and disjunctive flashbacks, a situation worsened by the traumas of racism.

As an interracial couple, the Hills were marginalized in their effort to be taken seriously as they went public with their experience. Their attempt to prove something happened was met with resistance by a white supremacist culture that also was skeptical about the likelihood of extraterrestrial life.

Rather than render the arcane as a mode of transcendental escapism, the book is an effort to understand ordinary, quotidian states of consciousness by exploring unsettling extremes on the margins of consciousness. My interest in the margins of vision—in this case, my interest in a phantasmic alien encounter—is actually an effort to re-envision the center.

One of the poems in the book, "The Orb," dramatizes my brief, firsthand encounter with the arcane—a strange light in the sky, perhaps a UFO, that I saw as I returned from a failed attempt to visit the Hills' abduction site in 2012. I was staying at a hotel in Durham, New Hampshire, and over the course of four consecutive days, I tried to drive to the White Mountains for research that could help me capture the mood and tone of the abduction site for the book. The idea was inspired by a trip to Dallas I made in 2006, visiting the Texas School Book Depository and the Grassy Knoll as research for *Historic Diary*. As I did in Dallas, I wanted to write from the tactile experience of the historical landscape itself, absorbing the sensory detail around me so that I could imagine what the physical environment of the area felt like to the Hills. But while the trip to Dallas was relatively easy, a flight from Chicago and then a cab to Dealey Plaza, my efforts to drive to the Hills' abduction site were thwarted by an unfortunate stroke of bad luck: I was visiting New Hampshire during a week of incessant thunderstorms. Each time I tried to drive into the White Mountains, extreme weather caused me to turn back around and return to Durham.

My fifth attempt, the night of "The Orb," seemed different at first—overcast skies, but no hint of rain. The weather changed dramatically just a few miles into the mountains, when a flash storm struck. The pounding rain made visibility impossible, and I had to turn back around. As I drove back to my hotel, I resigned myself that I would not, after all, write a poem about visiting the Hills' alleged abduction site. I decided instead to write about trying and failing to drive there.

Little did I know the strange turn my poem idea would take as I neared Durham, driving on Route 108 as the latest thunderstorm cleared. Just a few miles from my hotel, I saw a bright dollop of light above me, a white orb, an oddly bulbous image—the likes of which I'd never seen in the sky before—flying from right to left in my field of vision. In the moment it took for the orb to move across the sky, I tried to rationalize it as an identifiably terrestrial object. Probably a helicopter, though I saw no tail outline or taillight. I didn't have time to think much further about it, though—as I gazed at the sky through my car's windshield, I nearly drove myself off the road. When I looked up again, the orb was gone from my field of vision. In my rearview mirror, I took note of the ditch I'd nearly driven myself into, a moment I dramatized in a parenthetical aside in "The Orb," emphasizing the danger of watching a luminous object in the sky while driving an automobile: "(now I know why / Barney Hill pulled their car into a picnic area)."

I don't care whether I saw an extraterrestrial craft that night, or whether it was instead an earthbound aircraft or an explainable trick of the light in the nighttime sky. Of course, I'd love to know if the truth really is out there, as the old *X-Files* tagline goes. When it comes to UFO sightings, however, I take the lead of journalist Leslie Kean and describe myself as an agnostic. I wish I knew definitively what I saw that night in the sky outside Durham, but I can't know for sure. In the absence of trustworthy proof that something happened, I have no other option but to abide in agnosticism.

I'm more interested in what the experience felt like, and how this mysterious occurrence generated an emotional foundation for the poem. In that instant, watching something mysterious flying above me, a shape and movement I'd never seen before in the sky, my frame of reference suddenly lapsed into a dizzying groundlessness. This conceptual vertigo recalled for me one of the most uncanny incidents in the Hills' abduction narrative—when their captors pulled down a star map from the wall of their ship that traced their expeditions and trade routes. Betty was shocked, bewildered, that she could not find Earth on the map. It must've felt like she was looking at a map of our world with North America missing. Earth was nowhere; her home planet no longer her central frame of reference. Betty could not reclaim the center until the aliens returned the Hills to their car. Yet, by then, the center had been transformed irrevocably by her strange experience on the spaceship. Despite the evidence of our senses, most of us, myself included, process our day-to-day experiences as if the ultimate frame of reference is always already our individual consciousness. The collapse of this illusion is frightening, of course, but it also can be inspiring as it deconstructs our preconceived boundaries of the known. The resulting disorientation can trigger a productive reconfiguration of our ways of seeing.

"The Orb" demonstrates the limitation of the familiar writing workshop dictum, "Write what you know." I find it more valuable to write with an eye toward what I *don't* know. To proceed from unknowing is unsettling and potentially destabilizing because it invariably leads to feelings of groundlessness and conceptual vertigo. But inhabiting an "I-don't-know-mind" or "beginner's mind," as it is often described in Zen Buddhism, prepares me to recognize moments of self-discovery when they arise in my writing. What to do when you look to the sky and see something that violates your foundational understanding of who you are, of who others are—of what should be up there in the sky and what is literally alien? Write about it. If I compose from what I already know, I'm preparing myself only to reconfirm the known. Instead, I'd rather confront the questions that arise, and the potential discoveries to be made, when my writing welcomes, in all its conceptual messiness, the mysterious and the arcane.

I'm not the only poet who's ever been drawn to arcana, or to a literally out-of-this-world muse. Two poems by Craig Raine and Robert Hayden come to mind as models for how extraterrestrial subject matter can deepen our commitment to earthbound realism and history. Exactly as its title suggests, Raine's 1979 poem, "A Martian Sends a Postcard Home," unfolds from the perspective of a Martian visitor to our planet describing the bizarre life practices of his inscrutable earthling subjects for the extraterrestrial folks back home. ("Model T is a room with the lock inside— / a key is turned to free the world // for movement," Raine's Martian explains in one of my favorite moments in the poem.) "A Martian Sends a Postcard Home" was a staple in my writing classes as an undergraduate in the mid-1980s. In my early years as an instructor, I also turned to it frequently as a writing prompt for my students. *Write a poem describing your commute to class today*, began one of these early assignments, *but tell the story from the perspective of a Martian persona writing a dispatch to his home planet*. As a prompt grounded in the allure of the arcane, it is an exercise in vision, encouraging students to defamiliarize their environment in order to see the ordinary world from strange new frames of reference.

Hayden's 1978 "[American Journal]" demonstrates how the arcane can produce a politically urgent heightening of everyday lived experience. Hayden's poem is written from the perspective of an alien anthropologist reporting back to his superiors—"The Counselors," as they're called—an effort, like that of Raine's speaker, to make sense of the strange earthling subjects of his study. Raine's exercise in vision and perspective becomes, in Hayden's poem, a vital critique of American racism—perhaps more incisive because it is seen from the perspective of an interstellar stranger, a curious extraterrestrial ethnographer who, in disguise, observes the traumatic effects of racism from a vantage that lies beyond our earthbound subjectivity: "the imprecise and strangering / distinctions by which they live   by which they / justify their cruelties to one another." Hayden's speaker comes to us from a "strangering" beyond, so far outside our frame of reference that the drama of the poem pivots on its ability to disrupt its readers (Hayden's use of the graphic design of the page, the caesuras he creates with blank spaces in the middle of lines, contributes to this disruption). Hayden crafts an urgent call for social change from this defamilarized space beyond our Earth-centered frame of reference—a "strangering" we usually encounter in science fiction extrapolation. "[C]rowds gathering in the streets today for some / reason obscure to me," Hayden's extraterrestrial writes of a street protest and ensuing police riot: "noise and violent motion / repulsive physical contact   sentinels   pigs / i heard them called   with flailing clubs rage." The arcane inhabits a speculative realm that is an extrapolation of our real historical moment. It is a space for an intensified realism, even though on the surface it might seem like transcendental fabulism (UFO phenomena) or non-literary trash (the rise and fall of the PTL empire).

Any discussion of the poetics of the arcane would be incomplete without a look at Jack Spicer, who famously declared in his June 13, 1965, Vancouver Lecture that his writing was the dictated product of "Martian" dispatches from outer space. Spicer was speaking of a figurative muse-like voice—he did not truly believe that literal Martians were talking to him. As committed as he might be to making the world strange in his body of work, his poems speak to us from demarcated terrestrial boundaries. Spicer's "Martians," instead, are a metaphor for poetry's necessary encounter with what he calls "the Outside," the margins of rote day-to-day thought and vision. For Spicer, the Outside is a liminal space where we have an opportunity see the world more completely, without the editorializing interference of a conscious mind that would domesticate the mysteries of vision in order to make them less unsettling. Spicer claims that poetry emerges from a range of Outside sources, in forms he variously describes as anonymous radio transmissions, ghostly visitations, invasive parasites, and "Martians," to name a few.

Embracing the enigmatic and esoteric can feel like summoning the supernatural, insofar as it requires the poet to be a vessel for a mysterious force that can destabilize our familiar, often stale, habits of vision and speech. But I would argue that the arcane only seems otherworldly because it disrupts our conventional ways of seeing; that is, the arcane occupies such an uncanny space in our consciousness that we cannot find adequate language to describe it—beyond approximating it as "strange" or "alien." The star map that Betty Hill allegedly was shown on board the saucer is literally out of this world, but as a metaphor for vision, it is no different than any other moment when our seemingly stable frame of reference is disoriented by its presence in foreign terrain: we are temporarily othered in the presence of the arcane, and this can feel like an invasion of our consciousness. However, the imagination is not a passive process. As Spicer says in the June 13 lecture, "You have to, as much as possible, empty yourself for this." To prepare the body to hear what the parasitic muse is actually trying to say, you must "empty yourself" of the conditioning voice that otherwise would garble the ghostly "Martian" transmission. Spicer's disruptive voices from the mysterious Outside can evade our consciousness unless we attune ourselves to the proper frequency of Outside speech. "You have to interfere with yourself," Spicer states in the same 1965 lecture, a reminder that we need to create an environment for re-envisioning our conventional ways of seeing before we can even hear the muse-like voices of the Outside.

Spicer's poetics of the Outside was on my mind when I composed "*The UFO Incident*," a sestina in *Proof Something Happened* inspired by a 1975 made-for-television movie about the Hills' experience. As I researched the cast of the film, I discovered that veteran character actor Barnard Hughes, the Hills' psychiatrist in the movie, also played the role of a nervous con man named Jack Spicer in a 1971 episode of the television detective series *Cannon*. The sestina was an early-draft mess until I found the *Cannon* episode in Hughes's Internet Movie Database (IMDB) television filmography. At that point, I knew that Hughes's 1971 Jack Spicer had to appear in the poem, as a nod to Spicer, the poet for whom "Martians" were among the voices central to his writing process. Was my research discovery an example of the Outside communication that Spicer emphasized was crucial to his writing process? Seeing Jack Spicer in Hughes's filmography startled me. But it could've been nothing more than a strange coincidence had I not been open and vulnerable to this arcane detail as I drafted the poem. I had permitted the Outside to "interfere" with me, to inject Spicer's Martian poetics explicitly in the work, and this created the conditions for my composition of the poem. Eventually, I built the entire sestina around an opening stanza in which Spicer, the television con man, evokes Spicer, the poet indebted to metaphorical Martians.

(Here's another occult-like incident that possibly "emptied" me so that I could be receptive to the Hughes/*Cannon* moment in the poem. It was summer 1985. I was nineteen and on the verge of a breakdown after a psychologically brutal year. One night, as I walked upstairs in a house I shared with two other students, I suddenly heard the voice of actor William Conrad, the man who played Detective Frank Cannon in the television series, calling my name. It's the only time in my life I've heard voices—a consequence, I imagine, of the daily anxiety attacks of that period in my life, the constant stream of the stress hormone cortisol. I don't claim with certainty that Conrad's voice came to me from Spicer's Outside. But I wonder if this auditory vision momentarily prepared me—"emptied" me, as Spicer would say—so that I would be able to hear Conrad and Spicer speaking from the esoteric margins three decades later as I wrote "*The UFO Incident.*")

As I mention earlier, the advice to "Write what you know" reaches its limit in the presence of the arcane. To be sure, writing what you know can be empowering as a validation of the truth and wisdom of your experience. But I would suggest instead that the most productive work comes from those moments when we write what we don't know—when, to channel Spicer again, we "interfere" with the boundaries of the known and attune our ears to what is being spoken to us from the arcane "Outside."

More specifically, these are moments in which we interfere with the part of ourselves that doesn't want to step out of the boundaries of common sense, that fears getting lost in the dark wood of unknowing. On the surface, it might seem counterintuitive to welcome an alien frame of reference, a destabilizing angle of vision, as we sit in front of the blank screen ready to write. But if we are to discover new ways of seeing the world, as good writing can help us do, then we might need to loosen our grip on the most familiar, ordinary parts of our consciousness: "You have to, as much as possible, empty yourself for this," Spicer says. The arcane doesn't have to reside in outer space. Instead, it can be found among us, planted firmly on planet Earth—in gossip, scandal, and soap opera kitsch, to name a few possibilities—an affirmation of the wisdom and insight we can find when we celebrate, rather than domesticate, our most eccentric curiosities.

Or, to put it another way, more personally: my writing takes shape in the abandoned televangelist theme park of the imagination, my mother on the phone, secretly donating what little money we had, believing in an otherworldly, redemptive spirit that Jim and Tammy Faye Bakker channeled from beyond the same dull round of what we already know. When I sit down to write, I try not to anticipate what I'll find in this theme park, just as I had no idea I'd see an orb in the sky outside Durham after another failed attempt to reach the Hills' abduction site. My work begins with a desire to write myself out of what I know—to immerse myself in a vulnerable, arcane unknowing.

CHAPTER SEVEN

Coming Back to the Page 101 Times

Nearly every morning before breakfast, I sit on a cushion in my living room for fifteen to twenty minutes and do nothing goal-oriented or accomplishment-based. I just sit and breathe, refocusing my attention as much as possible on my in-breaths and out-breaths. I try to notice, rather than follow, the thoughts chattering in my head—the random memories, feelings, ideas, and to-do lists that arise with each breath.

I began a daily meditation practice in 1994, but I only started to understand the relationship between meditation and writing three years later, during a memorial ceremony for Allen Ginsberg at Northeastern University. The event was held in the Physics Department's largest lecture hall, where the previous semester I saw poet Robert Creeley read to a packed house. One of my graduate school colleagues, Lorianne, who also was a Zen teacher, began the Ginsberg event by placing a bell on a table at the front of the room. She rang the bell, then stepped away. Once it stopped resonating, she approached the table and rang it again. She backed away once more. Then she returned to the table and, amid the fading echo of the bell, rang it a third time. I was intrigued by how she planned to integrate the bell into her Ginsberg talk, but at the same time, my mind was too distracted to pursue this question in any depth. Three times my impatient mind heard the bell, and three times I failed to focus my attention on the sound and its echo. *Should I buy a salad or a cup of yogurt for lunch? How many papers can I grade before my 2:15 class? How many students did today's assigned reading? What's my backup plan, in case only a few of them did the work?* I was gone, miles it seemed, from the lecture hall where the bell was still resonating. My distracted narratives about lunch and my upcoming afternoon class seemed to extend for a significant length of time, but they actually hadn't even outlasted the echoes of the third bell.

Lorianne waited for the final after-sound to diminish, then stood still for an extra few beats of silence. Then she bowed—once to the bell, and again to the audience.

"Some of us probably experienced the bell as a pleasant sound," she eventually said, "and some of us just flat-out didn't like it. Or maybe you even heard the bell as music and identified it as a D note. No matter how the sound of the bell reached our ears, we all categorized it in some way. A 'good' or 'bad' sound, or a particular musical note—or maybe a metaphor to unpack before I started speaking. But what might be more interesting is to reflect on what arose in the ear *before* our minds labeled the sound as 'good' or 'bad.'"

Lorianne paused, as if to give us time to recollect what the bell sounded like in that moment right before each of us named the sound in language.

"The best poets try to linger on the raw sound itself in that split-second before the mind categorizes it," she continued. "Allen Ginsberg was one of those poets."

Lorianne's bell dramatized for me poetry's impulse to say the unsayable—poetry's noisy silence that resides in, as she described it, "that split-second before the mind categorizes" what it has heard. She was inviting us to consider poetry's uncanny ability to speak what cannot be put into words, what cannot always be communicated logically within the constraints of basic, everyday social discourse. It was a demonstration of the contentious (but generative) relationship between mind and language. As writers, we know that sometimes the words unloose themselves in fluid, suggestive phrasing that creates an immediate environment of self-discovery. But most of us have experienced the opposite, too, when the mind is so bent upon judging our words—so determined to control our words at the moment we speak or write them—that the imagination becomes its own worst enemy, listening only for whether the words, like Lorianne's bell, sound "good" or "bad" without hearing the noisy, non-conceptual silence in the mind as we write.

If I'm not careful, these moments when my mind sits in judgment of what I'm hearing, fixated on whether my language and phrasing are "good" or "bad," can lead to writer's block. The words don't seem to come. Or if they do, the writing itself is flat because I'm too distracted by my judgmental mind to actually listen to the sensations, tones, ideas, and feelings coming from my mind and body. Or I'm just too preoccupied to listen to myself at all, ruminating on the day's joys and slights, lost in internal narratives that allow me to escape the present by chattering about what the future will bring—anything to run away from the restlessness that arises when I try to stay focused on the present moment.

At a fundamental level, meditation practice doesn't demand that we think differently; nor does it suggest that we are thinking wrongly. Instead, it encourages us to observe our thoughts more than we do during our waking hours, when we tend to move through the world governed by our distractions. My meditation practice is not an effort to control the mind and body but instead to listen to it, to observe and be soft with it. The same holds true for my writing practice. I don't want to exert undue control over my words, but instead want to listen to them, to be gentle with them—to follow where the language wants to go, rather than forcing the words into preconceived notions about the form and content of what I am writing.

Ironically, as important as meditation practice has been for my writing, my first experience with it was rife with distraction. I was a third-year undergraduate student at Kent State University. A close friend had dropped by my apartment to see if I wanted to join him for that evening's meditation sitting at the Kent Zendo. A Zendo is a physical setting, usually a formal temple or meditation hall, where a trained Zen Buddhist teacher guides students through sessions of sitting meditation. In our case, the Kent Zendo was the Zen teacher's large, two-bedroom apartment in a courtyard building on the north side of our college town.

I'd been curious about sitting practice for a few years, and this was my first chance to try it. I sat comfortably on a meditation cushion on the hardwood floor with a group of seven others, including the teacher, in the Zendo's spacious living room. My body settled into what looked to me like the same quarter-lotus sitting position everyone else was in. I found myself easily following the Zen teacher's advice to breathe and take notice of my in-breaths as they touched my nostrils and my out-breaths as they tickled my upper lip. The eight of us sat in silence. I settled into a calm, abiding awareness of the moment: "right here, right now, just this," as my current Zen teacher likes to describe this feeling.

Everything changed just a few minutes into the session. The Zendo's next-door neighbor was a drummer, as it turned out, and he started practicing not long after I'd noticed that feeling of meditative calm pervade the room. Quite a distraction for me, but not because of the noises produced next door by a full drum kit (snare, bass drum, tom-toms, and cymbals). Instead, as a drummer and percussionist myself, I was preoccupied with judgmental evaluations of what the neighbor was playing. I could hear him attempting complicated snare-tom-bass triplet sequences. Then he'd stop, as if to gather himself, before resuming with familiar warm-up snare rudiments I'd learned when I first started playing the instrument. When he nailed a difficult rhythmic pattern, I felt a mixture of happiness for him and also jealousy, despite my confidence as a musician, as I allowed his success to make me feel self-conscious about my own limitations. As relaxing as it was for my first meditation experience to unfold with a drummer practicing next door—not so much for my fellow meditators, as they said later, during our large-group discussion—I found it impossible to observe my breathing while also sitting in judgment of the neighbor's musicianship. I permitted myself to be led around by my wandering thoughts, like a dog chasing a stick, instead of merely noticing them as a cat would watch, but not run after, the same stick. I was consumed by the drummer, expending most of my imaginative energy listening to him instead of noticing the rise and fall of my breath. To recall Lorianne's bell, I wasn't allowing the neighbor's drumming to reach my ears as the noisy, non-conceptual silence of raw sound—that is, as something my mind, for a split-second, did not try to fit into logical categories like "good" or "bad." I was obsessed, instead, with envious internal monologues every time his technique seemed better than mine, which, in turn, generated catty self-satisfaction when he made mistakes that led me to conclude I was, indeed, the superior percussionist.

·

I used my first-ever meditation session to prove to myself, at a stranger's expense, what a terrific musician I was. Buddhism describes this as "self-cherishing." It was easier to celebrate myself that day than to observe myself, easier to judge myself as a "good" first-time meditator and a "good" musician than to notice all that was, as usual, roiling inside me—all the mental chatter that distracted me from inhabiting, in mind and body, the room in which we all were sitting. My effort to stay grounded in the present ("right here, right now, just this") proved elusive as I sat on my cushion and nurtured my reactionary ego as a musician.

Once I stopped observing my breath, I lost the concrete sense of

my body in space, and my posture slouched. The Zen teacher period-
ically asked me to sit straighter as the night went on, because, as he
reminded us, allowing your back and stomach to go slack leads to brain
fog and sleepiness during meditation. I tried to follow his guidance.
But I lapsed into a quarter-lotus slouch each time I directed my atten-
tion to the neighbor's drumming and, in doing so, created extended
self-cherishing narratives in my head about my musicianship.

It's a wonder I ever made it back to the everyday consciousness
of the present moment that evening at the Zendo. Still, I look back
on that night with fondness for how I struggled. I was consciously
aware of the conflict I was experiencing as I tried to meditate, and
I felt a palpable constriction of mind and body as I obsessively fol-
lowed my thoughts about the "good" and "bad" sounds the neigh-
bor was making. Yet I also felt an expansive sense of possibility in
those flashes of insight when I observed, without indulging my edi-
torializing, judgmental mind, a wider range of what was happening
in the room in which we sat—the raw sounds of the drums and cym-
bals as they reached my ears; the shifting of my fellow meditators on
their cushions; and, as always, the incessant rattle of free-associative
thoughts in my head. My struggle with meditation that night taught
me an important lesson that would be reinforced years later by Lori-
anne at the Ginsberg ceremony: the imagination flourishes in that
split-second before the editorializing and judgmental mind intrudes.
With my attention diverted by my critiques of the drummer next door,
I learned more about my distracting mental habits than if I'd slipped
into the blissed-out transcendental state that our stereotypes of med-
itation had taught me to expect that evening. Reflecting on the strug-
gle to stay focused helped me understand much later how precise the
phrase "meditation practice" is. Meditation is a practice that, like any
other, needs to be performed regularly before our self-consciousness
about it drops away and the act itself becomes second nature. Our
writing is no different. We are doing a *writing practice*, a mind-train-

ing practice that, with persistent, sustained effort, becomes easier to perform as we begin to recognize that our editorializing, self-conscious mind can become a hindrance if we allow it to take control of the imagination. Applying meditation to writing involves resisting our urge to control our thoughts and force them into language we feel is "right" or "acceptable." Meditation practice helps us, as writers, observe more clearly what we see in the imagination and to render, without self-judgment, the details of what we see.

But given the enormous distractions of daily life, applying meditation to the writing process might seem anything but simple, especially when we're in the midst of a creative block. In such moments, I try to remind myself that writer's block is not a failure of the imagination. Instead, to evoke Lorianne's bell again, writer's block often occurs when my editorializing mind gets in the way of my imagination's need to linger in that non-conceptual, silent moment before I've imposed language on the sound and labeled it as "good" or "bad" (or as a perfect D note). As I'll discuss later in this chapter, meditation can intensify our ways of seeing, leading often to a heightened perception that can break through writer's block by facing and redirecting the tremendous energies of our daily distractions.

My effort to embrace and reroute distraction is inspired by strategies taught by my first meditation teacher, Andrew Weiss, a lay practitioner of Insight Meditation and a student of the late Vietnamese Zen master Thich Nhat Hahn's *Tiep Hen* School (the Order of Interbeing). Weiss would instruct us to accept distraction as an inseparable texture of the landscapes of our everyday, ordinary minds. Distraction is produced by the same mind that can quiet distraction, Weiss taught. "If you are distracted from your breath 100 times," he would say, "just make sure you come back 101 times." In my own individual writing practice, such an approach nurtures the imagination, helping me recognize distractions that threaten the writing process. More important, it suggests that I can redirect distraction by facing it head-on, rather

than surrender to the chattering internal monologues that character-
ize so much of waking life. Meditation can encourage us as writers to
experience distraction as an inevitable phenomenon, an extension
rather than a disruption of our creative process. If we are distracted
from the page 100 times, then the imaginative focus enabled by med-
itation practice can help us return to the page 101 times.

.

I realize this chapter could sound at times like an abstract excursion
into the philosophy of language. But my hope instead is to bring the
complicated workings of our writers' minds down to earth. Medita-
tion can be a practical method for disentangling the thoughts and
counter-thoughts that seem to ricochet constantly in our heads. It is
a pragmatic aspect of my writing practice that helps me understand
the relationship between the imagination and language.

In the spirit of pragmatism, I want to introduce a basic, guided
breathing experiment you can apply to your own writing. It can be
especially helpful during periods of writer's block. I've adapted it from
a meditation exercise in Buddhadāsa Bhikkhu's 1988 book, *Mindful-
ness with Breathing: A Manual for Serious Beginners* (revised and reis-
sued in 1996). I created my own version of Buddhadāsa's exercise for
those moments when I'm stuck in a creative block. You don't need a
Zendo or even a meditation cushion to give this a try. Just find a com-
fortable place to sit in your home. Then close your eyes and breathe.

Step One: Observe Your Breath
Begin by paying attention to your breath, noting in particular the dif-
ference between your long and short breaths, and focusing on the
sensation of your in-breath touching your nostrils and your out-breath
tickling your upper lip. Try just to observe your breathing and not
attempt to control it. Knowing that a long breath relaxes the body and
a short breath can tighten the body, it's easy to succumb to the temp-

tation to exert your will upon your breath in order to force the body to relax. In such moments, instead of listening to what the body is telling us about its relative state of relaxation or anxiety—communicated to us through calm, longer breaths or tense, shorter breaths—we risk spending so much time trying to create the perfect breathing situation that we no longer can truly hear what the body is expressing to us about our state of mind. Much the same is true of our writing: if we allow the editorializing mind to control the writing process, we won't listen to what the imagination is trying to express. Instead, we'll spend the writing session trying to force the "perfect" words from the mind, which often results in writing few words at all. But our writing practice trains us to become keen observers of the outside world, a form of sight-training not much different than the ear-training required for musicians. This power of observation can be refocused internally on the mind and body, helping us notice and follow our breaths in the first stage of this exercise.

Step Two: Anchor Your Breath
Once you feel comfortable locating your in- and out-breaths, a process that requires a few minutes of sitting still, you can direct your concentration to either the nostrils or the upper lip. Whether you choose to focus on the in-breath touching your nostrils or the out-breath tickling your upper lip matters less than choosing one location to fix your attention on. This spot on the nostrils or the lip will serve as an anchor, a stable reference point, for your focus of attention. Buddhadāsa describes this anchor as the "guarding point" of one's breath: once you find a location to anchor your breath, he writes, "guard that point as the breath passes in and out. The mind [...] stays right at that point and contemplates the breath as it goes in and out." This guarding point helps us observe, but not succumb to, the inevitable distractions that arise when we try to sit still. Using the guarding point as an anchor ensures that even if you're distracted 100 times from

your breath, you'll likely return 101 times to the physical, tactile location that you're "guarding" at your nostrils or at the top of your lips.

Step Three: Notice the Images that Arise

Fixing our attention on the breath makes us more alert. We begin to notice the images arising in the mind and, in turn, we become more sensitive to particular images that are recurring. As you feel more and more at ease with the process of following your breath, you can choose one of these images and associate it with the anchor you've located at your nostrils or upper lip. (When I do this exercise, I put no boundaries on what this image can be—only that I want myself to be comfortable enough with this image that, as I'll discuss shortly, I can manipulate it and write about it.) In this moment, you can trust the ordinary, image-making impulses of the human mind. "The mind merely inclines in a certain way and the image arises by itself," Buddhadāsa writes in *Mindfulness with Breathing*. Whether you're feeling prolific or stuck, the mind's image-making capabilities seem immune to obstacles. After all, even when we're mired in writer's block, we dream at night in vivid, often highly detailed images. No matter what your state of mind might be, images never fail to arise during this stage of the exercise, and one of these images will persist in the foreground of your imagination, inviting your full attention. Allow yourself several minutes to sit with this image and observe it. Try to examine it, as if the image were an object you're turning in your hand and seeing from multiple angles of vision.

Step Four: Manipulate One of the Images

Once you feel that you've explored the image in detail, gently push yourself to change it into something else. Perhaps you'll want to transform its shape or color, or maybe you'll feel like redirecting its range of motion. It's important to approach this stage of the meditation with looseness. Pick just one particularly vivid element of the image to transform. This stage is not about choosing the "right" element of the object to manipulate, as if you were listening to Lorianne's bell ring over and over until you found the perfect tone or pitch to write about. Instead, it's an effort to make something new from an image that emerged from your distracted mind. The goal is to be at ease with the imagination so that you can guide it to be more active than it usually is during a period of writer's block. Do everything you can to feel comfortable changing the image, knowing that your mind *can* see sharp images even when you're struggling to produce new writing, and that these images can be revised and remade by the active imagination engaged in ordinary perception.

Step Five: Write About the Image You Manipulated

The final step in this exercise is the most basic and fundamental stage of the process: write in your journal for five to ten minutes, asking yourself only to describe the image as you saw it, and altered it, during the meditation. It's important to emphasize that the image you've located at the anchoring point of your breath—the image you manipulated during the guided breathing—might not find its way into a piece of finished writing. Try not to worry about whether or not the object of your imagination will be "good enough" to build a piece of writing around. All that's requiring of you is to describe in detail the image that arose in your mind.

.

This five-step guided breathing meditation serves as a reminder for me that the art of writing is, at its core, a matter of seeing the world as clearly as possible and then transcribing for our readers what we are seeing. When I break down the writing process to this essential foundation, I think of poet and novelist Lewis Warsh's account of the artistic breakthrough he experienced after reading his poems in public for the first time, which he describes in *Piece of Cake*, a collaborative memoir with Bernadette Mayer: "My poems were still dense language games dotted with occasional moments of true feeling, but within the year I was able to see how by just putting down what I did and who I saw every day I could never be at a loss for something to write about." The writing I produce in the final stage of this exercise is often purely descriptive, a documentation of what was created by the generative, image-making powers of the imagination. It reinforces for me that readers are more likely to discover themselves in the minute particulars of my ordinary life than in the high-minded puzzle-making of "dense language games dotted with occasional moments of true feeling."

Even though meditation is often represented in North American mainstream media as something exotic, it's the most ordinary day-to-day activity we can do. Assuming that our lungs are healthy, nothing could be more basic, or even mundane, than the observation of our in-breaths and out-breaths while images arise in our minds. This particular exercise emphasizes for me that the most powerful tools we have for breaking writer's block are the same elements that create the block through their own vulnerability to distraction: the triad of body, speech, and mind, which, in Buddhism, are vehicles that, depending on the seriousness of our practice, can lead us to wisdom or distress. Through guided breathing and an active imaginative engagement with the images that arise in our minds, we can open our fields of perception to include distraction itself, suggesting that our vulnerability to *distraction* can be transformed into a vulnerability to *perception*. I often turn to this guided breathing meditation in periods when, for whatever reason, I find myself trying to control my imagination as it shapes my thoughts and feelings into words.

·

I was writing this chapter during a semester in which I taught Meditation and Poetics, a graduate craft seminar for creative writing students. One evening around midterm, as I brought the class to an end,

I introduced a final exercise that, unknown to me at the time, would exert a direct influence on my own writing.

I walked through the classroom, stopping at each student's chair at the seminar table, asking each to pick one of Brian Eno and Peter Schmidt's famous "Oblique Strategies" cards that were spread out, face-down, in my hands. The Oblique Strategies deck consists of 103 palm-sized, white glossy pasteboard cards with one or two sentences printed on them in basic black text. The text written on each card offers an aesthetic challenge—sometimes pragmatic, other times downright orphic—to help artists apply new frames of reference to their work-in-progress. Helpful, suggestive cards I've picked for myself in the past, for my own writing, include: "Give the game away"; "Emphasize the flaws"; "Mute and continue"; "Do nothing for as long as possible"; "Go outside. Shut the door"; and "Feed the recording back out of the medium," to name a few. I remember it was easy to go outside and shut the door when I picked that particular card a few years ago; recently, though, I recall struggling to discover how to "Feed the recording back out of the medium" on the occasion I chose that card. I never figured out what it meant to "Feed the recording back out of the medium," but then again, the Oblique Strategies cards are not designed to be "figured out." The cards suggest random, often nonlinear ideas for thinking through the revision process. The process of struggling to comprehend the text of the "Feed the recording back out of the medium" card led me to discover new revision pathways in the piece of writing I was working on at the time. "The path is the goal," as we often say in the mindfulness and meditation community. While perhaps we say this too much, the phrase is a helpful axiom, all the same, for how to use the Oblique Strategies cards. The goal is not for me to decode the more esoteric cards, but to apply the cards to my writing practice and trust that this process will open up new paths of perception as I revise.

The discussion prompt for my students that night was basic:

1) pick one of the Oblique Strategies cards spread face-down in my hands; 2) reflect on it for a few minutes; then 3) write about how they might apply the card to a piece of writing they were currently revising. After this short period of writing, we went around the room and students read one-by-one the revision ideas inspired by their randomly chosen card.

I participated in the class activity, too. Given how cryptic the Oblique Strategies deck can sometimes be, the card I picked this night was remarkably straightforward:

"What are you really thinking about just now? Incorporate."

What was I *really* thinking about? All my thoughts, it seemed, were directed toward how to orchestrate tonight's class discussion—to help students generate strategies to subvert the control-freak internal editors who live inside our imaginations. I was in the middle of teaching my class, so I wasn't consciously reflecting on my own writing. Or so I thought.

What are you really thinking about just now? Incorporate.

I am thinking about "control."

Incorporate it.

This card emphasized that my thoughts right now, in the present moment, are worthwhile in themselves and have artistic potential in themselves. It also encouraged me to *incorporate* what I'm thinking about right now—to bring it literally *into* the *corpus*, or the body of my writing. The Oblique Strategies card I picked that night in class suggested to me that "control" was a crucial concept I needed to address as I revised this final chapter. Driving home that night, still reflecting on the question of control, I decided to begin this chapter with the story of Lorianne's bell—to write about her bell as a metaphor for evading our over-controlling conscious minds as we write.

Back home that night, in my building on the north side of Chicago, one of my neighbors held open the elevator door for me as I rushed from the mail room. I appreciated her help. I was having a difficult

time holding several pieces of mail, three magazines, and two pack-
ages without dropping anything.

"Are they something special?" she asked, pointing to the parcels
tucked under my left arm. "Something you've been waiting for?"

"The larger one is addressed to my wife. I'm not sure what it is.
But this one," I said, gesturing toward an Amazon package, "is some-
thing I really need for an essay I'm writing."

It was the newest edition of *Mindfulness with Breathing*, from 1996,
which replaced the 1988 edition that Shelly took with her when we
divided our books during the divorce. Shelly had studied with Bud-
dhadāsa's translator, Santikaro Bhikku, and that particular edition of
the book held great meaning for her. I knew I needed to reread *Mind-
fulness with Breathing* as I finished this chapter, and I was grateful the
new edition had just arrived.

"What's the book about?"

"It's on meditation," I said. "Actually, on breathing and medi-
tating."

"I once had a friend who meditated and he learned how to levi-
tate," she said.

We both laughed. The elevator doors opened onto my floor.

"What I'm talking about in my essay is much more down to earth,
I hope."

It's as down to earth as noise and silence. Since my first artistic
training was in music, it's natural for me to think in terms of sound
and music when I'm writing poems. This is no great revelation, of
course, given poetry's origin in song. Whether harmonious or discor-
dant, poetry is to language as music is to noise. "Which is more musi-
cal, a truck passing by a factory or a truck passing by a music school?"
avant-garde composer John Cage asks in *Silence: Lectures and Writings*.
Cage's question might seem like a Zen koan, an esoteric riddle. But
I hear it as an invitation to experience more deeply the relationship
between noise and music, language and poetry, silence and speech.

It's a way of feeling the silent, kinetic din of Lorianne's bell between the moment it's been rung and the moment I've begun to categorize the sound of its ringing in language. Cage's question is a reminder to listen to the noisy silence of my mind and body as I write—and to listen without the interference of editorializing preconceptions.

What are you really thinking about just now? Incorporate.

New Titles in the Chapter One Series from Marsh Hawk Press

CREATIVITY: WHERE POEMS BEGIN | **BY MARY MACKEY**

A meditation on how the sources of creativity emerged from a vast, wordless reality and became available to a poet. As such, it is not only a memoir; it is an exploration of the power and process of becoming a poet. What is creativity? Where do creative ideas come from? What happens at the exact moment a creative impulse is suddenly transformed into something that can be expressed in words? To describe creativity is extraordinarily difficult because the moment of creation comes from a place where language does not exist and where the categories that determine what we see, hear, taste, and feel are not immediately present. In our daily lives we tend to live on the surface, unaware of the complexity and richness of what lies below. Poetry creates itself, bubbling up from the depths until it reaches that part of our brains that transforms consciousness into words. Poetry chooses the poet. The poet did not choose it. This book is a journey to that place where all poems begin.

PLAN B: A POET'S SURVIVORS MANUAL | **BY SANDY MCINTOSH**

If you're a poet, how are you going to survive if you can't get a teaching job? You need a Plan B if you want to put food on the table, wear shoes without holes in the soles, and stop living with roommates before you turn sixty. Taking us on a witty, fascinating, no-holds barred romp through his own experiences in the world of commercial writing and publishing, McIntosh reassures us that it is possible to have a successful career as a poet while holding down day jobs that make us better writers. "*Plan B* is a wonderful book, an important book, a book aspiring writers of fiction and poetry should read." —David Lehman, Editor, *The Oxford Book of American Poetry*. Series Editor, *The Best American Poetry*.

WHERE DID POETRY COME FROM: SOME EARLY ENCOUNTERS | BY GEOFFREY O'BRIEN

A memoir in episodes of some early encounters—with the spoken word, the written word, the sung word—in childhood and adolescence, encounters that suggested different aspects of the mysterious and shapeshifting phenomenon imperfectly represented by the abstract noun "poetry." From nursery rhymes and television theme songs, show tunes and advertising jingles, Classic Comics and Bible verses, to first meetings with the poetry of Stevenson, Poe, Coleridge, Ginsberg, and others, it tracks not final assessments but a description of the unexpected revelations that began to convey how poetry "made its presence known before it had been given a name."

About the Author

Tony Trigilio's recent books of poetry are *Proof Something Happened* (Marsh Hawk, 2021), selected by Susan Howe as winner of the Marsh Hawk Poetry Prize, and *Ghosts of the Upper Floor* (BlazeVOX [books], 2019), the third installment in his multivolume cross-genre project, *The Complete* Dark Shadows *(of My Childhood)*. His books of poetry also include *Inside the Walls of My Own House* (BlazeVOX, 2016), *White Noise* (Apostrophe Books, 2013), and *Historic Diary* (BlazeVOX, 2011), among others. His selected poems was published in Guatemala in 2018 by Editorial Poe (translated by Bony Hernández). He is the author of two books of criticism, *Allen Ginsberg's Buddhist Poetics* (Southern Illinois University Press, 2012) and *"Strange Prophecies Anew"* (Fairleigh Dickinson University Press, 2000). He is editor of *Elise Cowen: Poems and Fragments* (Ahsahta Press, 2014) and co-editor of *Visions and Divisions: American Immigration Literature, 1870-1930* (Rutgers University Press, 2008). Trigilio co-founded the poetry journal *Court Green* in 2004, and from 2017-2021 was an associate editor for *Tupelo Quarterly*. He is a Professor of English and Creative Writing at Columbia College Chicago.

Titles From Marsh Hawk Press

Jane Augustine *Arbor Vitae; Krazy; Night Lights; A Woman's Guide to Mountain Climbing*

Tom Beckett *Dipstick (Diptych)*

William Benton *Light on Water*

Sigman Byrd *Under the Wanderer's Star*

Patricia Carlin: *Original Green; Quantum Jitters; Second Nature*

Claudia Carlson *The Elephant House; My Chocolate Sarcophagus; Pocket Park*

Lorna Dee Cervantes: *April on Olympia*

Meredith Cole *Miniatures*

Jon Curley *Hybrid Moments; Scorch Marks; Remnant Halo*

Joanne D. Dwyer *RASA*

Neil de la Flor *Almost Dorothy; An Elephant's Memory of Blizzards*

Chard deNiord *Sharp Golden Thorn*

Sharon Dolin *Serious Pink*

Joanne Dominique Dwyer *Rasa*

Steve Fellner *Blind Date with Cavafy; The Weary World Rejoices*

Thomas Fink *Zeugma, Selected Poems & Poetic Series; Joyride; Peace Conference; Clarity and Other Poems; After Taxes; Gossip*

Thomas Fink and Maya D. Mason *A Pageant for Every Addiction*

Norman Finkelstein *Inside the Ghost Factory; Passing Over*

Edward Foster *A Looking-Glass for Traytors; The Beginning of Sorrows; Dire Straits; Mahrem: Things Men Should Do for Men; Sewing the Wind; What He Ought to Know*

Paolo Javier *The Feeling is Actual*

Burt Kimmelman *Abandoned Angel; Somehow; Steeple at Sunrise; Zero Point Poiesis; with Fred Caruso The Pond at Cape May Point*

Basil King *Disparate Beasts: Basil King's Beastiary, Part Two; 77 Beasts; Disparate Beasts; Mirage; The Spoken Word/The Painted Hand from Learning to Draw/A History*

Martha King *Imperfect Fit*

Phillip Lopate *At the End of the Day*

Mary Mackey *Breaking the Fever; The Jaguars That Prowl Our Dreams; Sugar Zone; Travelers With No Ticket Home; Creativity*

Jason McCall *Dear Hero*

Sandy McIntosh *The After-Death History of My Mother; Between Earth and Sky; Cemetery Chess; Ernesta, in the Style of the Flamenco; Forty-Nine Guaranteed Ways to Escape Death; A Hole In the Ocean; Lesser Lights; Obsessional; Plan B: A Poet's Survivors Manual*

Stephen Paul Miller *Any Lie You Tell Will Be the Truth; The Bee Flies in May; Fort Dad; Skinny Eighth Avenue; There's Only One God and You're Not It*

Daniel Morris *Blue Poles; Bryce Passage; Hit Play; If Not for the Courage*

Gail Newman *Blood Memory*

Geoffrey O'Brien *Where Did Poetry Come From; The Blue Hill*

Sharon Olinka *The Good City*

Christina Olivares *No Map of the Earth Includes Stars*

Justin Petropoulos *Eminent Domain*

Paul Pines *Charlotte Songs; Divine Madness; Gathering Sparks; Last Call at the Tin Palace*

Jacquelyn Pope *Watermark*

George Quasha *Things Done for Themselves*

Karin Randolph *Either She Was*

Rochelle Ratner *Balancing Acts; Ben Casey Days; House and Home*

Michael Rerick *In Ways Impossible to Fold*

Corrine Robins *Facing It; One Thousand Years; Today's Menu*

Eileen R. Tabios *Because I love you I Become War, The Connoisseur of Alleys; I Take Thee, English, for My Beloved; The In(ter)vention of the Hay(na)ku; The Light Sang as It Left Your Eyes; Reproductions of the Empty Flagpole; Sun Stigmata; The Thorn Rosary*

Eileen R. Tabios and j/j hastain *The Relational Elations of Orphaned Algebra*

Tony Trigilio: *Proof Something Happened; Craft: A Memoir*

Susan Terris *Familiar Tense; Ghost of Yesterday; Natural Defenses; On Becoming a Poet* (editor)

Lynne Thompson *Fretwork*

Madeline Tiger *Birds of Sorrow and Joy*

Tana Jean Welch *Latest Volcano*

Harriet Zinnes: *Drawing on the Wall; Light Light or the Curvature of the Earth; New and Selected Poems; Weather is Whether; Whither Nonstopping*

YEAR	AUTHOR	TITLE	JUDGE
2004	Jacquelyn Pope	*Watermark*	Marie Ponsot
2005	Sigman Byrd	*Under the Wanderer's Star*	Gerald Stern
2006	Steve Fellner	*Blind Date with Cavafy*	Denise Duhamel
2007	Karin Randolph	*Either She Was*	David Shapiro
2008	Michael Rerick	*In Ways Impossible to Fold*	Thylias Moss
2009	Neil de la Flor	*Almost Dorothy*	Forrest Gander
2010	Justin Petropoulos	*Eminent Domain*	Anne Waldman
2011	Meredith Cole	*Miniatures*	Alicia Ostriker
2012	Jason McCall	*Dear Hero,*	Cornelius Eady
2013	Tom Beckett	*Dipstick (Diptych)*	Charles Bernstein
2014	Christina Olivares	*No Map of the Earth Includes Stars*	Brenda Hillman
2015	Tana Jean Welch	*Latest Volcano*	Stephanie Strickland
2016	Robert Gibb	*After*	Mark Doty
2017	Geoffrey O'Brien	*The Blue Hill*	Meena Alexander
2018	Lynne Thompson	*Fretwork*	Jane Hirshfield
2019	Gail Newman	*Blood Memory*	Marge Piercy
2020	Tony Trigilio	*Proof Something Happened*	Susan Howe
2021	Joanne D. Dwyer	*Rasa*	David Lehman
2022	Brian Cochran	*Translation Zone*	John Yau